Progressives and Prison Labor

SERIES ON OHIO HISTORY AND CULTURE

Series on Ohio History and Culture
Kevin Kern, Editor

Barney Taxel and Laura Taxel, *The Lake View Cemetery: Photographs from Cleveland's Historic Landmark*

Joseph Congeni, MD, with Thomas Bacher, *Cleveland's Bitter Pill: A Diagnosis of Injured Title Dreams and Die-Hard Fans*

Steve Love, *The Indomitable Don Plusquellic: How a Controversial Mayor Quarterbacked Akron's Comeback*

Robert J. Roman, *Ohio State Football: The Forgotten Dawn*

Timothy H. H. Thoresen, *River, Reaper, Rail: Agriculture and Identity in Ohio's Mad River Valley, 1795–1885*

Mark Auburn, *In the President's Home: Memories of the Akron Auburns*

Brian G. Redmond, Bret J. Ruby, and Jarrod Burks, eds., *Encountering Hopewell in the Twenty-first Century, Ohio and Beyond. Volume 1: Monuments and Ceremony*

Brian G. Redmond, Bret J. Ruby, and Jarrod Burks, eds., *Encountering Hopewell in the Twenty-first Century, Ohio and Beyond. Volume 2: Settlements, Foodways, and Interaction*

Jen Hirt, *Hear Me Ohio*

S. Victor Fleischer, *The Goodyear Tire & Rubber Company: A Photographic History, 1898–1951*

Ray Greene, *Coach of a Different Color: One Man's Story of Breaking Barriers in Football*

John Tully, *Labor in Akron, 1825–1945*

Deb Van Tassel Warner and Stuart Warner, eds., *Akron's Daily Miracle: Reporting the News in the Rubber City*

Mary O'Connor, *Free Rose Light*

Joyce Dyer, *Pursuing John Brown: On the Trail of a Radical Abolitionist*

Walter K. Delbridge and Kate Tucker, editor, *Comeback Evolution: Selected Works of Walter K. Delbridge*

Gary S. Williams, *"No Man Knows This Country Better": The Frontier Life of John Gibson*

Jeffrey A. John, *Progressives and Prison Labor: Rebuilding Ohio's National Road During World War I*

For a complete listing of titles published in the series, go to www.uakron.edu/uapress.

Progressives and Prison Labor

Rebuilding Ohio's National Road During World War I

Jeffrey Alan John

The University of Akron Press
Akron, Ohio

All new material copyright © 2022 by the University of Akron Press
All rights reserved • First Edition 2022 • Manufactured in the United States of America.
All inquiries and permission requests should be addressed to the Publisher,
The University of Akron Press, Akron, Ohio 44325-1703.

ISBN: 978-1-62922-140-3 (hardback)
ISBN: 978-1-62922-141-0 (ePDF)
ISBN: 978-1-62922-209-7 (ePub)

A catalog record for this title is available from the Library of Congress.

∞The paper used in this publication meets the minimum requirements of ANSI/NISO z39.48–1992 (Permanence of Paper).

Cover image: Ohio Department of Transportation construction photos collection, Ohio History Connection Archives, Series 2203 AV. Cover design by Amy Freels.

Progressives and Prison Labor: Rebuilding Ohio's National Road During World War I was typeset in Minion Pro and printed on sixty-pound white and bound by Bookmasters of Ashland, Ohio.

Produced in conjunction with the University of Akron Affordable Learning Initiative. More information is available at www.uakron.edu/affordablelearning/

In memory of Cyrus,
who lay curled at my feet
while I wrote this book.
We miss you.

Contents

Foreword	ix
Notes about the Images	xi
Introduction	1
I. The Road	4
II. Good Roads	11
III. War Roads	27
IV. Forty Thousand Trucks	34
V. Five Million Bricks	44
VI. Sledgehammers and Picks	55
VII. Victory Declared	70
VIII. The Last Brick	75
IX. Settling Accounts	80
X. Winners and Losers	87
Epilogue	97
Acknowledgments	100
Notes	102
Bibliography	112
Index	120

Foreword

HARDSCRABBLE RESIDENTS OF southeastern Ohio's rolling hills know they live atop blue-gray gold. In the early 1800s the settlers who lived in these Appalachian foothills—and before them the indigenous inhabitants of the area—found clean, pure clay that they fired in ovens fueled by the abundant wood and coal of their area. Family practices taught each generation to create bowls and vessels for their homesteads, and by the late 1800s the crafts evolved a wide variety of products: bricks, reddish-brown and durable; simple earthenware pots that sat on the front porches of rough wood cabins and tabletops in warm, smoky kitchens; and then artistic goods featuring sprigging of creamy white, delicate leaves on vines on cobalt blue backgrounds, or colorful, incredibly intricate country scenes preserved in glaze. The industry thrived in communities such as the village of Crooksville, known as the "Pottery Capital of the World," while the more substantial cities of East Liverpool and Steubenville, accessible to Ohio River flatboats, acquired fame for their ubiquitous wares. Kitchen cabinets today still hold fine dinnerware manufactured in eastern Ohio by Homer Laughlin Company, Hall China Company, or Knowles, Taylor and Knowles.

Residents of the area delight in telling this fable about their resource: when engineering crews came through the area to dig the path of the National Road, known locally as "the Pike," neighbors took advantage of the situation. The excavations often revealed the valuable blue-gray mineral, so at night people from the surrounding countryside surreptitiously wheeled in with pick, shovel, and barrow to remove buckets of the stuff, leaving gaping holes behind them in the dirt roadway. Wagon masters on the Pike, the first significant east–west land transportation

Potholes in the National Road, circa 1910. *Ohio Department of Transportation construction photos collection, Ohio History Connection Series 2203AV.*

artery of the growing infant United States of America, had to become adept at dodging those craters.

Over time horse-drawn conveyances evolved into motorized vehicles. The somewhat greater speed of the machines made an uneven surface even more treacherous, as drivers wove between interruptions they knew as "potters' holes." The term naturally became shortened to "potholes," the bane of modern motoring commuters.[1]

Notes about the Images

PICTURES THAT ARE more than a century old present special problems for the historian working with visual communication. Provenance of visual works of historical interest is important, and confirming the authenticity of many images reputed to be from the 1918 National Road project has been at best challenging and at worst debatable. The photos reproduced in this book that exist in archives as physical copies, while in mostly good condition, lack any identification other than random scrawled marginal notes, probably references to long-lost negative files or office folders. A number of images have been preserved thoughtfully as digital files, but most include minimal identification or dates.

The historical work photos in this book present good examples of issues the visual historian encounters. The Ohio History Connection Archives and Special Collections include more than 1,600 Ohio Department of Transportation (ODOT) photographic prints and postcards, and many construction photos are identified as from the National Road project. The Ohio History Connection's National Road/Zane Grey Museum also holds a collection of work photos reputed to be from the 1918 National Road project. ODOT separately has a large digital image archive that can be polled using search terms, with results identified by location, year, and often some description. In addition, historian David Adair has assembled an outstanding collection of photos that trace Guernsey County history.

Many pictures in the Ohio History Connection Archives also show up in the ODOT collection, but with differing years (1918, and 1917 or 1912, respectively) and locations (the ODOT online collection identifies its images as mostly from Franklin County). Over the intervening hundred years some images must have been misidentified, but which ones?

At issue specifically for purposes of this book are assorted images held in ODOT collections that depict Black men at road-building work. The digital photos made available through ODOT show Black workers in civilian clothes, with rolled-up blue jean cuffs, working in view of what appear to be overseers. The men pour gravel between thick concrete curbs, per National Road specifications and perhaps most important, thousands of bricks are stacked behind them. However, some of the images include margin notes specifying dates in October 1912 and Franklin County, Ohio. A search of the Columbus *Dispatch* of that autumn confirms both error and corrections: the September 29, 1912, edition of the paper includes a half-page photo feature reproducing the work photos in question, thus establishing the date as September, not October, and also confirming the Franklin County location. The newspaper also explains that the county had set aside a short stretch of road south of Columbus for an "experimental road" to test brick, concrete, and bituminous pavement. According to author Wayne E. Fuller, in 1912 Congress released $10,000 to each state for such roadway experiments,[1] and the newspaper account says that the work crews included men from the Ohio State Penitentiary.[2]

The Ohio History Connection Archives also hold many old ODOT photos, including originals of the ODOT images available online. More than 1,200 photos, in files dated between 1907 and 1920, depict early roads in deplorable condition and men working to pave those roads. Numerous images show Black men at work shoveling gravel or applying tar. Most of these photos are undated, but the subject matter provides hints: because the Ohio legislature declined to use prison labor on road projects until the 1912 "experiment," then a few years later only reluctantly on the National Road 1918 rebuilding project, the source must be one of these two projects. Bricks are stacked in some photos, but not all, and concrete, not allowed in the 1918 National Road reconstruction, is being poured and smoothed in some images. Convict workers in the confirmed 1912 photos appear to be somewhat better dressed, in matching uniforms and hats, while others, likely those photographed in 1918, are wearing scruffier clothing. Unfortunately, none of the photographs includes identification of the subjects. Thus, the convict workers remain nameless to this day.

Introduction

A HOLIDAY ATMOSPHERE greeted Ohio Governor James M. Cox and his traveling group in Cambridge, Ohio, the morning of March 13, 1918, almost a year after the US entered World War I. Schools had been dismissed, and citizens packed the common pleas courtroom of the county courthouse "so thoroughly that several women fainted and had to be carried out," one newspaper reported.[1] Ohio Highways Commission president Allen R. McCulloch, a Cambridge resident who stood in the front of the courtroom, introduced a slate of speakers including state Attorney General Joseph McGhee, Council of National Defense Chief Engineer Raymond Beck, and the governor. In a "ringing appeal," Governor Cox linked patriotism to his request for the cooperation of the community in a massive wartime road-building project that would run right through Cambridge.

"All must lay aside politics," he said. "We won't have political parties, or even religion if the Kaiser wins." He assured the crowd that funds would be available for the needed work, but labor concerned officials most. "The state has the means and machinery to do the work, but workers are lacking," Cox said. "The newspapers should make it uncomfortable for the man who stands on the street corners and will not work.

"All we ask of you is hearty cooperation. Make it possible to get laborers."[2]

The governor didn't mention that he added the earnest request because he and his entourage already had discussed the labor-supply problem in detail. "This work must be completed this fall," Cox announced. "Plans have been made to have men confined in the penitentiary at Columbus and also at Mansfield to work on the road."[3]

According to the plans, "hundreds" of convicts would be employed. The prisoners would work in squads of fifty, unshackled and without prison dress. "The men selected will be those eligible for early parole, and those whose likelihood of escape is small, for few guards will be used," reported the Zanesville *Signal*. "In each case those who will be sent to work on the roads will be men who have volunteered for the service. The statement of Warden P. E. Thomas that the work is necessary to help the country in the war evoked much enthusiasm at the prison." Then, seemingly hidden as an afterthought, the *Signal* added, "The majority of the prisoners used will be negroes [*sic*]."[4]

At the time, the Ohio State Penitentiary had a population of 1,996 prisoners, of whom 306 were "colored," to use the language of official state documents.[5] With Black numbers such a small fraction of the total prison population, who or what decided that skin pigmentation would determine whether a prisoner would be selected for the road labor crews? The answer lay in racial beliefs of prison administrators and Ohio politicians, and in society's prevailing modes of thinking of the time. These notions accepted and twisted reforms that were part of the baggage of the social and political movement called the Progressive Era.

We recognize now the warped sensibilities, but an important distinction must be made here between incarceration in Ohio of the early twentieth century versus the brutal Jim Crow methods of the South, as detailed in Douglas Blackmon's comprehensive and Pulitzer Prize-winning *Slavery by Another Name*. Blackmon describes a post-Reconstruction history in the South of Black men arrested on trumped-up charges such as vagrancy, with the sole intention of contracting them out as unpaid laborers. In part because of those conditions, tens of thousands of African Americans moved north after 1910 in the Great Migration, and this book enters the situation at that point in time. Prisoner assignment to National Road labor happened after the fact of arrest in Ohio, and although there is no way (short of examining individual court records) to confirm the legitimacy of the incarcerations,[6] it must be noted that Ohio law did not allow contract labor; the men working on the road were in effect paid employees of the state, albeit poorly paid. Contemporary newspapers also reported the volunteer status of at least the first prisoner groups taken to the Pike, although it's equally possible that the accounts drew from the

Introduction 3

notes of gullible reporters quoting the warden, or that the cell-bound convicts recognized road work as an opportunity for fresh air and open skies. Whatever the reason, ultimately about two hundred of the three hundred African American prisoners in the Ohio Penitentiary were sent out as labor on the road.

The following pages tell the story of Ohio's multi-million-dollar National Road reconstruction campaign in the spring and summer of 1918. The project can be seen as the capstone in Ohio of the Progressive Movement's substantive years of 1900 to 1920, when social and hard sciences were applied to improve the lackluster lives of the common man and woman. But this eight-month road-building undertaking, spurred by national fervor during World War I, also illustrates well how racism and old-fashioned politics permeated the Progressive Era.

In order to provide the necessary context, this book's narrative reaches back into the history of the Midwest to include such notable personalities as land speculator Ebenezer Zane, US Representative Albert Douglas Jr., and Ohio Governor James Middleton Cox. Within the actual road construction, hundreds of Ohio convict laborers comprised the mostly Black worker corps, but ironically only those who escaped had their names recorded for history.

The entire undertaking accomplished a great deal in its time and place, but very little survives. For about a dozen years communities situated on the Pike east of Zanesville, Ohio, enjoyed a brick-paved roadway, a vast improvement over the previous rutted dirt surface, but in the 1930s the state government repaved and straightened the National Road so that only a few lengths of winding original brick surface remain. Thus literally buried, the road-building project that consumed all of southeastern Ohio in the spring and summer of 1918 has fallen out of memory. Yet in the years motor cars rolled on it, the bricked route served as an exemplar of the waning Progressive Era, providing efficient transportation routes to the impoverished foothills of the Appalachian Mountains and linking new interstate motorways.

I

The Road

IN THE FALL of 1768, leaders of the Iroquois Six Nations yielded to pressure from white land speculators and settlers and signed the Treaty of Fort Stanwix, near present-day Rome, New York, ceding what is now West Virginia and Kentucky to the British. Open lands beckoned, and Ebenezer Zane recognized opportunity.

Born October 7, 1747, in a Virginia settlement on the far western edge of the expanding British colonies, Zane descended from adventurous stock. By age twenty-one he yearned to acquire his own property for a growing family that included his wife Elizabeth McColloch, daughter of a well-known western Virginia family, and his infant daughter Catherine. Ebenezer ventured west with his older brother Silas and younger brother Jonathan and established "tomahawk claims" by marking four hundred acres of trees on both sides of the Ohio River at its confluence with Wheeling Creek. Ebenezer and his siblings cleared land, then erected a stockade with nine-foot wooden walls and a blockhouse that they named Fort Fincastle. By 1770 they had brought families, some Black people the family had enslaved, and livestock to the few cabins that would become Wheeling, West Virginia.[1]

However, the Shawnee people refused to cooperate with the Fort Stanwix treaty because they still asserted ownership of the area as hunting grounds. During conflict with them in 1774, Zane earned the rank of colonel as a disbursing agent for the British military. A few years later he

The Road

supported the American colonies in their rebellion, which prompted combined British and their Shawnee and Mingo allies to launch repeated attacks on his river settlement. In 1782, British and Native American belligerents besieged the garrison, by then renamed Fort Henry in honor of Virginia's Governor Patrick Henry. During that grim episode, Zane's sister Betty became the stuff of legend.

Her grandson, Zane Grey, described the event years later in his book *Betty Zane*. He recounted how, in the midst of the siege, she volunteered to fetch gunpowder stored sixty yards distant at Ebenezer's cabin. The attackers, surprised when they saw a young woman leave the outpost, withheld gunfire until they realized her mission. According to Grey,

> ...The bullets were raining about her. They sang over her head; hissed close to her ears, and cut the grass in front of her; they pattered like hail on the stockade-fence, but still untouched, unharmed, the slender brown figure sped toward the gate. Three-fourths of the distance covered! A tug at the flying hair, and a long, black tress cut off by a bullet, floated away on the breeze. Betty saw the big gate swing; she saw the tall figure of the hunter; she saw her brother. Only a few more yards! On! On! On! A blinding red mist obscured her sight. She lost the opening in the fence, but unheeding she rushed on. Another second and she stumbled; she felt herself grasped by eager arms; she heard the gate slam and the iron bar shoot into place; then she felt and heard no more...[2]

Betty survived to deliver the ammunition, having suffered only a slight wound. The Shawnee and British forces eventually withdrew from the battle, fought almost a year after Lord Charles Cornwallis surrendered His Majesty's forces at Yorktown. Historians consider the Fort Henry battle the last conflict of the American Revolution.

Ebenezer Zane represented Ohio County at the United States constitutional convention of 1788. Ever the land speculator, he became familiar with personalities in the new US government and used his connections as he looked westward into the Ohio Country. In a 1795 letter to his "acquaintance" James Madison, then an influential member of Congress and adviser to Thomas Jefferson, he requested that his son-in-law John MacIntyre be appointed agent over "Western Lands" along the Scioto River.

"If a Land Office is Actually Opened, or Military Warrents to be Exe[c]uted his knowledge of those parts of the Western Country may perhaps not Only be of service to him Self But to those Gentlemen holding Military Warrents Who may incline to have them Executed," Zane wrote. "[I] take the Liberty of recomending Mr McIntyer to your notice With respect to Assistance & particularly for information respecting the disposal of those Lands [sic]."[3]

In 1796 Congress granted Zane a permit to build a road across Ohio to the "western country" and then to Kentucky, exchanging his surveying expenses for land grants of one mile square each where the road crossed the Muskingum, Hocking, and Scioto Rivers. Thenceforth called Zane's Trace, the route he and his brothers cut out of the wilderness from Wheeling to the banks of the Ohio River opposite Limestone, Kentucky, merely widened a trail used by deer and indigenous people, but it was the first such route in the Ohio Country, and the only major road in Ohio until the War of 1812. Zane used the properties at the rivers as profitable ferry crossings, one of which, on the Muskingum River, eventually became a town named Zanesville, the county seat and largest city in Muskingum County today.

Zane's Trace was a rudimentary ridgetop path suitable at first for travel only by foot or horseback. Sections tracked over steep hills, but as the only route to the west, it became deeply rutted, making progress difficult for settlers.[4] One of the Ohio legislature's first actions after the territory was admitted to the Union in 1803 was to provide funding to widen the road from Wheeling to Zanesville.

Meanwhile, the infant federal government in Washington began to take notice of potential commerce in its western reaches. Albert Gallatin, a Swiss-born land speculator who became first a member of Congress and then treasury secretary under President Thomas Jefferson, proposed a grand scheme to link all the former colonies by land routes and canals. This philosophy, promoted by Jefferson's new Democratic-Republican political party, espoused a sentiment that major roads to and through the Ohio Country would bring more settlers to western lands and help increase trade. When Jefferson acquired the vast Louisiana Purchase territory, the West became a major part of the growth strategy, despite Gallatin's concerns about excessive cost, and in 1806 Congress authorized the "Act to Regulate the Laying Out and Making a Road From Cumberland, in the State of Maryland, to the State of Ohio." This route headed northwest from Baltimore, Maryland, toward Zane's settlement at Wheeling.

The Road 7

Actual construction of the new route, using an up-to-date crushed-stone macadam process, began in 1811. The road met the Ohio River in 1818, and Congress proposed that tariffs could fund the nation's internal improvements, including an extension of the Cumberland Road beyond the river. Zane's old friend James Madison, who opposed government-funded road building, vetoed the plan in one of his last acts as president, although in 1820 Congress appropriated $10,000 to survey land for a route from Wheeling to the Mississippi River. Finally in 1825 Congress granted $150,000, provided by sale of land in Ohio, to build the road from Wheeling to Zanesville. Surveyors used Zane's Trace as their template, and by 1830 road construction crews had arrived in Zanesville. Three years later the road reached fifty-five miles west to Columbus, the state capital, and by 1838 the National Road was another fifty miles west in Springfield, Ohio.

For a few years, the Road—variously known as the National Road, the Cumberland Pike, or simply the Pike—was fabulously successful. According to Pike chroniclers Glenn Harper and Doug Smith, "A single year in 1833 recorded thousands of wagons, coaches and carriages, riders on horseback and immense droves of livestock."[5] Contemporary National Road historian A. B. Hulbert reported, "An old stage driver in eastern Ohio remembers when business was such that he and his companion Knights of the Rein and Whip never went to bed for twenty nights, and more than a hundred teams might have been met in a score of miles."[6] Hulbert offered this detail:

> This was the real life of the road—coaches numbering as many as twenty traveling in a single line; wagon-house yards where a hundred tired horses rested overnight beside their great loads; hotels where seventy transient guests have been served breakfast in a single morning; a life made cheery by the echoing horns of hurrying stages; blinded by the dust of droves of cattle numbering in the thousands; a life noisy with the satisfactory creak and crunch of the wheels of great wagons carrying six and eight thousand pounds of freight east or west.[7]

The National Road spurred the construction of taverns every few miles and enabled the growth of Midwestern communities including Zanesville, Cambridge, and Bridgeport. As the Ohio population grew, the National Road linked the new Ohio state capitol of Columbus with commercial and political centers of the East.

Always more of a commercial route than a touring road, however, the Pike soon faced trade competition from new forms of transportation and technologies. The same day that ribbon-cutting ceremonies opened the National Road at St. Clairsville, Ohio, on July 25, 1825, work began on the Ohio and Erie Canal about ninety miles west, at Licking Summit near present-day Heath, Ohio. That waterway and the Miami and Erie Canal crossed the Road, and in total more than one thousand miles of canals eventually linked the Great Lakes and the East with commerce on the Ohio River. Marketers found transportation via the water courses a bargain: flour trundled along the National Road cost $25 a ton, whereas on canal boats the same product cost $3 a ton.[8]

Within a few years the iron horse made both the National Road and the canals obsolete. Beginning with horse-drawn rail cars in the mid-1830s, railroads soon linked the rest of the country with territory that the National Road had made accessible only a score of years before. New rail technologies dazzled politicians who held the purse strings: a committee of the US House of Representatives, debating the merits of continued funding of National Road construction around 1838, estimated news carried by rail could move from Baltimore to Columbus in a mere twenty-three hours, to Indianapolis in forty-two hours, and to the terminus of the Road in Vandalia, Illinois, in fifty-four hours.[9]

By the 1850s, when the Baltimore and Ohio Railroad crossed the Allegheny Mountains, passengers and freight could travel relatively cheaply and at speed. Whereas stagecoach travelers could count on a ten- or twenty-mile journey from one tavern to another in a day, and passengers on a canal packet pulled by a mule could float along all day at three miles an hour, early steam locomotives could roll easily between major cities in a day's time. And in the late nineteenth century, beginning with a short line that paralleled the National Road between Granville, Ohio, and Newark, Ohio,[10] light rail interurban cars made travel even easier. For a few cents, passengers could hop aboard a comfortable electric vehicle and be whisked along at speeds up to fifty miles per hour between communities. In some areas, rural customers could wait by the side of the rails and flag down passing interurban cars, often sharing the ride with packages or mail. By the height of its popularity in 1910, light electrified rail made a web that linked thousands of miles throughout the Midwest.[11]

The Road 9

Meanwhile, the National Road and other surface paths became more of a nuisance than a public resource. Its early success contributed to the Road's failure—as countless narrow wagon wheels destroyed the layers of gravel. As early as 1822, in an effort to get users to pay for road repair, Congress authorized gates and tolls. President James Monroe vetoed that bill as an unconstitutional intrusion into commerce of the individual states, but Congress continued to balk at using taxpayer dollars for maintenance of the highway. In 1836, House Bill 64 shifted money originally appropriated for the National Road to building a railroad west of Columbus, Ohio, calculating that while it would cost more to build a rail line, maintenance of the highway would far exceed that of the railroad.[12]

Instead, the federal government passed ownership of the National Road to the states it crossed. The states, in turn, gave responsibility for maintenance and repair to the individual counties the Road served, and according to Hulbert, "Farmers who lived on the route of the road engaged in the [repair] work when not busy in their fields, and for their labor and the use of the teams received good pay."[13]

Local toll systems provided those dollars: a horse and rider at a Pennsylvania gate could expect a charge of four cents, a score of sheep or pigs cost six cents, and a stagecoach twelve cents. Toll gates were encountered about once every twenty miles in Pennsylvania, and once every ten miles in Ohio. Tolls collected at the stops amounted to more than $60,000 (in 1840s dollars) per year while the Pike was in its heyday, but by 1877 the income dwindled to a mere $288.[14]

That year, the Ohio state legislature allowed the counties to poll their voters on the question of whether to continue the toll road system or allow free travel on the Road. "[If] a majority of all those voting on said question shall vote yes, it shall be the duty of said commissioners to sell gates, toll houses and any other property belonging to the road to the highest bidder, the proceeds of the sale to be applied to the repair of the road," the law stated.[15]

Apparently then, as now, few voters wanted to increase their own taxes. By 1900 the old road had fallen into such disrepair that it had become in many places nothing more than a country lane with a crumbling, muddy track. One observer noted that whereas countless "wheelmen," "drivers," and horse riders once utilized the Pike as a thriving commercial artery, it had now become rutted, shredded by potholes, and in at least once location washed out by a meandering stream. The roadway was shrinking in girth, too: over the years farmers who owned fields that bordered the Cumberland Pike often encroached, squeezing the path from an eighty-foot-wide right-of-way to a narrow lane.[16]

II

Good Roads

CONTEMPORARY ACCOUNTS DESCRIBE Albert Douglas Jr. as something of a Renaissance man. A graduate of Kenyon College and Harvard Law School, he had a deep interest in history, especially the Civil War, and enjoyed the works of the poet Robert Blake. He loved fishing and the outdoors, according to those who knew him in his hometown of Chillicothe, Ohio. Wanderlust must have affected him as well: his quest for knowledge led him several times to Blake's Scotland, the European continent, and to Civil War battlefields of the eastern United States. He and his family enjoyed esteemed status: society pages of the local newspaper cooed about the well-spoken Douglas and his fashionable wife, Lucia, in their appearances at cotillions of the community.

Descendants as far back as his great-grandfather, an officer in the Revolutionary War, and his grandfather, a veteran of the War of 1812, practiced law. Although Albert Sr. detoured to become a prominent Chillicothe doctor, Albert Jr. returned to the law, serving a law firm in the community for nearly thirty years, during which time he represented clients ranging from utility companies to an African American man who sued a local school board in order to allow his two daughters to enroll. Douglas served two terms as Ross County prosecutor, earning accolades from local Republicans as "a man any Republican can vote for with pride and satisfaction; a clean, able, conscientious and honorable man, who is

Congressman Albert Douglas Jr.,
Library of Congress

known and respected throughout the state."[1] They elected the Republican Douglas in 1906—and again in 1908—to the US House of Representatives from Ohio's 11th district.

Glowing local stories recognized Congressman Douglas's spirit of adventure. He became an early adopter of the horseless carriage, writing in one journal that "independence and the feeling that you are not imposing on a good horse, as well as the lust for 'pushing on'... are elements in the pleasure of traveling by automobile."[2] In the summer of 1910, after new route guides—the precursor to road maps and modern GPS software—became available, he, Lucia, and their chauffeur embarked on a motor tour. Their new Ford Model T runabout took them from Washington, DC, north through New England, across upstate New York, into Cleveland via the shores of Lake Erie, west to Elyria, and then south to his home in Chillicothe. Upon their arrival home, the *Scioto Gazette* of his hometown marveled at the two-thousand-mile journey, observing that "Mr. and Mrs. Douglas return browned by the sun, but well and rested."[3] Douglas said he found New England and New York roads in good shape, but Ohio's roads were "the worst they encountered on the whole trip."[4]

That November a Democratic wave swept Albert Douglas out of office with the rest of Ohio's GOP officeholders. A lame duck session of the 61st Congress kept Douglas in Washington until August the following year,

Good Roads

and when he, Lucia, and their driver departed the nation's capital, his motoring experience and intense interest in history prompted the former representative to embark on another visionary travel adventure. "We had bought our railroad tickets, reserved berths in the sleeping car and expected to proceed home to Chillicothe by the conventional railroad train," he wrote. "But when I suggested to my wife that instead of shipping our motor car we should ride home in it over the old National Road, she readily agreed."[5]

Douglas and Lucia found that their Ford, which they fondly named "Betsy," could manage about one hundred miles per day on the National Pike. He reported solid pavement in portions of the road in the eastern leg of their trip, although some Appalachian Mountain ascents sorely tested their vehicle. One steep climb particularly earned his disdain: "We found the road up Big Savage [mountain] . . . one of the worst on the whole trip," he complained, "and a disgrace to whomever is responsible for its condition. For this there might be some excuse if it were comparatively unused, but we found it on that Saturday afternoon thronged with teams [of horses]. The stones out of which the old road was constructed lay loosened amid the sand and dust, and through them 'Betsy' had to fairly [*sic*] plough her way." The travelers endured an uncomfortable half-hour struggle in the hot afternoon sun that day, but from the summit they enjoyed "the glorious view to the west and southwest, of meadows, fields, woods and piled up mountains."[6]

After an evening at a roadside inn and a day's drive later, the group wistfully put the mountain scenery to their backs and rolled into Wheeling. Douglas crossed the Ohio River "from which Ebenezer Zane blazed his famous Trace," and noted that Ohio terrain smoothed into rolling countryside. A day later they arrived in Chillicothe, and within months Douglas, a trustee of the Ohio Archaeological and Historical Society, posted in the society's journal a detailed account of their trip that opened eyes in Washington, DC, and state capitols along the old route. "The National Road today as a way of travel," he said, "may be described by the old phrase 'good, bad, and indifferent.' In spots it is excellent, and in spots it is execrable."[7]

With that article, Douglas confirmed his membership in one aspect of a new spirit of reform across the United States. In campaign literature of 1904 and 1906 he had proudly aligned himself with President Theodore Roosevelt, under whom the nation threw off late nineteenth-century Gilded Age politics of big enterprises directed by an anointed elite. Guided by Roosevelt's "Square Deal," government reined in business monopolies, enacted laws that protected workers, and in general adopted policies that encouraged new scientific research, technology, and efficiency intended to improve the lives of citizens. Roosevelt thus became a spearhead for what was becoming known as the Progressive Movement.

Progressive advocacy of transportation technology to advance the common good included a national crusade in support of better roads. Progressive efficiency required that initially bicycles and buggies, then horseless carriages, should rise out of the standard mud and gravel paths onto better pavements. By the beginning of the twentieth century, the US Department of Agriculture's small Office of Road Inquiry began to systematically examine and promote the nation's roads. Author Craig Colten, in his chapter "Adapting the National Road to New Technology," explained that the Progressives used a methodical approach. "With support from influential bicyclists, and initially the railroads, the Office of Road Inquiry sent engineering teams across the country to perform road-building demonstrations and thereby disseminate the information they had gathered," wrote Colten.[8]

Bicyclists were especially vocal, and their increasing numbers spurred an organized lobbying effort called the Good Road Movement. Popular support for the two-wheeled hobby had congealed as early as 1880, when bicycle manufacturers and users met in Rhode Island. There they created the League of American Wheelmen, which spread across the country and even published its own magazine, *Good Roads*. Eventually more than twenty state-level good road associations urged government action to improve crumbling pavements, which were considered inefficient and wasteful. At first, the movement pedaled uphill against federal legislative tradition dating to President Madison's veto of government support for the National Road project, but by the late nineteenth century, rural citizens—who had gotten used to a system of free postal delivery that struggled over crumbling rural roads—joined the movement.

Albert Douglas advocated with others in Congress for improved postal delivery roads. He recalled President Madison's belief that accord-

James M. Cox. From *Cox—The Man*, by Roger W. Babson; *Project Gutenberg. Public domain photo by Mathew D. Wheaton*

ing to the Constitution, an organized system of internal improvements should have been the province of the individual states. Douglas, however, did not agree that local funding should be a blanket condition, adding a historic caveat: "The power 'to establish post offices and post roads' with the powers necessarily incident thereto was invoked then, as some of us are trying to invoke it now, to secure help from the National Treasury for our roads over which pass the free rural mail routes," he wrote.[9]

A colleague in the Ohio congressional delegation provided even more strident support for post roads. James Middleton Cox, a wealthy newspaper publisher elected in 1908 to represent Ohio's Third District (Dayton and its environs), almost immediately joined the pro-road caucus. "I was a strong believer in the parcel post," Cox remembered later in his autobiography, but he found that others were not so inclined. For example, the National Wholesale Hardware Dealers Association actively opposed legislation to improve roads for rural mail routes because, they argued, more efficient delivery of merchandise to farmers would allow them to stay home while commerce in towns and villages withered. Cox recalled how they soon saw the error of their thinking, however: "It was not long until automobiles and the movies stimulated a volume of travel to the villages."[10]

Like Douglas, Cox was an early adopter of the horseless carriage. Unlike Douglas, Cox owned a patrician top-of-the-line 50 hp Stoddard-Dayton, which he enjoyed using in his first campaign for a House seat. "Indian Summer in the Miami [River] Valley is something to stir the soul of the poet, and I enjoyed driving through it," Cox commented.[11] He would canvass his district around Dayton by car during the day, then visit community meetings in the evening. More seasoned politicians advised him against it, recalling that a candidate for state legislature had lost an election because the politician's automobile scared the horses of potential constituents. In one incident during his own 1908 campaign, Cox reported, his motor car came up on a horse pulling a buggy. The frightened animal "did everything but climb a rail fence," and a local politician traveling with Cox feared they had lost the votes of the buggy driver, a minister, and his entire flock of congregants. The buggy driver merely laughed; Cox won the election despite his use of the threatening new transportation technology.

Both Douglas and Cox claimed the appellation "Progressive" in their campaigns, but whereas Douglas used the term merely to align himself with the popular themes of Republicans Theodore Roosevelt and William Howard Taft, Cox embraced a whole slate of ideas that by 1910 had earned the official title "Progressive." "All in all, the two Congresses of 1909–1913 in which I sat were an interesting and profitable school of public affairs," he recalled in his autobiography. "These years witnessed the eclipse of the standpat conservatism represented by the Old Guard leaders about Taft, and the growth of great new progressive forces—a change which I heartedly approved and so far as I could assisted."[12]

Cox came by notions of a desire to improve the life of the common person authentically. He had been born in Jacksonburg, in rural southwestern Ohio, in 1870, the youngest of seven Cox children. His stern father, Gilbert Cox, ran a spare family farm, and young Jimmy Cox only knew "a life of drudgery…hard work in season and out" on the farm. His father knew no other way, holding young Jimmy out of school each fall until the corn had been shucked.

"From early morning until late at night boys were kept busy," Cox biographer Roger Babson reported. The lifestyle apparently made the young Cox serious and taciturn. According to Babson, the only recreation for the young man consisted of evenings at Shafer's, a local store where Jimmy and other boys played outside and sometimes ventured indoors to watch locals play checkers. "All the residents remember Cox as a boy," Babson wrote. "When he got into Shafer's store, he would either be discussing with the men political problems, or else would be in one corner, under the old kerosene lamp, with his head buried in a good book."[13]

Good Roads 17

"Like most other children of the period, I owed much to the readers of William Holmes McGuffey," Cox remembered in his autobiography. "I went through these in order, from the first to the fifth, and they not only made me a master of many classic selections of English and American literature, but aroused in me a thirst for more reading in the masterpieces of our tongue." He also boasted of skill in mathematics and the social sciences, "because we were thoroughly drilled in them."[14]

Although teachers in his local little red brick schoolhouse found that young Cox possessed a good memory and energy, the skills necessary for rote learning, he admitted little patience as a true scholar: "While I was following the plow, I would often see one of the neighborhood schoolteachers starting off to work, and about four in the afternoon, while I still had long hours of toil ahead of me, I would see the teacher coming home," Cox wrote. "This spectacle might have given spur to my ambition to make a brief pedagogic career a stepping stone to something better."[15] Before he graduated, he took the state licensing exam for teachers and passed, to his surprise, so that he became a teacher in tiny Madison, Ohio, at age seventeen. He moved on to progressively larger institutions, eventually becoming the night school superintendent in nearby Middletown, Ohio, a small city situated halfway between Dayton and Cincinnati.

At the same time, he filled his Saturdays delivering all the printed copies of his brother-in-law's newspaper, the Middletown *Weekly Signal*. The work fascinated Cox; he admitted later, "My teaching experience was never more than an incidental pastime because, to use an old expression, printer's ink had moved into my blood."[16] The *Signal* soon became a daily newspaper with Cox as its only reporter, and after he scooped other local reporters on a train accident story near Middletown, the managing editor of the much larger Cincinnati *Enquirer* offered him a position as copy reader. The ambitious Cox accepted the invitation and stayed at the *Enquirer* for two years, during which time he moved up to a reporter's desk. One of his beats was the railroad, and unfortunately one of his stories ran afoul of Samuel M. Felton, a rail executive. The young reporter's story was accurate, according to both Babson and Cox, but it offended Felton, a thin-skinned man with no sense of public relations. To the dismay of Cox, the executive also happened to be a friend of the *Enquirer* owner, who had "some obligations" to the railroad official. Despite the support of the

Enquirer staff, Cox was moved to a new position. "He apparently felt that a moral principle was involved," Babson wrote. "If his story was untrue he was willing to be discharged, but if the story was true he believed that his editor should reprimand the railroad company for complaining. Apparently the editor did not agree with him, and thereupon Cox resigned."[17]

It was an unfortunate time for Cox to be between jobs. His wife, Mayme Simpson, was now pregnant with their first child. But as he wrote later in his autobiography, "What follows shows how a small event can have a vast cumulative influence on one's later life." Paul J. Sorg, a wealthy tobacco producer from Middletown, had just been elected to the US House of Representatives. One afternoon at the St. Nicholas Hotel in Cincinnati, while the new congressman compared notes with Judge John F. Neilan of the nearby community of Hamilton, Sorg professed a need for a private secretary. When Sorg said he preferred someone with a newspaper background, Neilan suggested Cox, who jumped at the chance after Sorg offered him the position.[18]

Washington, DC, impressed the young Cox. "The thrill that came to me when I first saw the Capitol and the White House at Washington must have been the same which comes to every youngster when he first steps on what to him has become sacred soil," he wrote. "Those were the horse and buggy days and in the White House stables were beautiful steeds and handsome equipages. Each member of the cabinet was alotted a fine team and a Victorian carriage."[19]

Sorg served only two terms in the House. He returned home in 1897 after he lost his enthusiasm for Washington when the Progressive agendas of Democrat William Jennings Bryan ascended. Cox meanwhile absorbed the personalities and strategies of the nation's capital, and as he returned home with Sorg he expressed regret as well as respect for what he had learned. "Not merely had I learned how Congress works and become acquainted with the practical side of politics–the logrolling and maneuvering on tariffs, rivers and harbors improvement, and other questions. I had also begun to appraise some of the forces underneath the politics of the day," he said.[20]

Cox, now twenty-seven, returned to Ohio with an itch to acquire a newspaper. The Dayton area attracted him because of its proximity to his home country, as well as its prosperity at the time, so when the Dayton

Good Roads   19

Evening News became available, he assembled the $26,000 purchase price by borrowing $6,000 from Sorg and a few other people, then added his own funds. Sorg persuaded Cox to sell shares in the newspaper operation at $50 a share, and the paper was opened in the Cox name on August 15, 1898. "[I was] too young to be running a newspaper," Cox admitted later.[21]

Cox proved to be a relentless and dedicated publisher who dragged a formerly moribund newspaper—now renamed the *Dayton Daily News*—out of a journalistic abyss. At first he headed a staff of four reporters, to which he added a woman society editor—Dayton's first—and the crew "worked like beavers," he recalled. Cox himself read and edited all the copy, wrote headlines, looked over page designs, and wrote editorials at night. Under his leadership the paper revamped a previously feeble advertising base by bargaining with local businesses and improving ad copy, and the *Dayton Daily News* slowly gained the grudging respect of Dayton's business leaders. "Dayton merchants speak well of Mr. Cox, but are not enthusiastic about him," one contemporary observer said. "They look upon him as a successful business man, although they don't especially like his paper."[22] Circulation rose from about 2,600 in 1898 to become Dayton's leading paper by 1900.[23]

Emboldened, Cox became a crusading publisher. First, he publicized the self-serving backroom deals of Dr. Joseph E. Lowes, a local Republican leader who subsequently sued Cox for libel but won a paltry $1 judgment in court. Then, in 1907, the *Dayton Daily News* confronted John H. Patterson, the eccentric founder and president of the National Cash Register Company, now known as NCR. Patterson had threatened to haul his enormous manufacturing plant out of Dayton after he failed to get permits for a railway spur into his property, but Cox called his bluff. Then the newspaper exposed Patterson's fascination with an English health guru and its deleterious effect on operations of National Cash Register, one of the nation's largest companies. "Libel suits fell like raindrops upon us," Cox commented, but the paper held its ground until Patterson eventually called off his legal reprisals. The battle became prime reading in the community, and by 1908 circulation had risen to about twenty thousand subscribers, while the Cox business operation grew to include improved presses and another newspaper, the *Springfield Daily News* in nearby Springfield, Ohio.[24]

His success in the newspaper business brought Cox to the attention of politicians. Edward W. Hanley, chairman of the county Democratic committee, recognized the weakened position of local Republicans who were riven by conflict between the progressive policies of President Theodore Roosevelt versus conservative business interests. "The leaders of our county suggested that I become a congressional candidate," Cox wrote later, observing that his thriving business plans at that time included construction of a new headquarters in downtown Dayton. "I was not easily persuaded," Cox said.[25]

Nevertheless, Cox sought and won the Democratic nomination as candidate for Ohio's third congressional district. As had been predicted, Republicans split into two camps, loyalists supporting the party and others who put forward an independent, making Cox an easy winner in the general election of 1908. He later admitted that campaign was his most his most enjoyable ever, with its pleasant motorcar tours of autumn in southwest Ohio during the day and town meetings at night.

However, he found he had to overcome one weakness: public speaking. A writer described his speaking style as lacking force, "and his manner was hesitating and uncertain."[26] Cox admitted that an early presentation before a political body exposed his trepidation. "I had memorized the speech and I will never forget the physical and mental torment that possessed me while I delivered it," he reported in his autobiography. "Inwardly I said to myself that if I ever got through I would never make another."[27] At the same time, friends took to stealing his written speeches, forcing Cox to speak extemporaneously. The effort worked; continued practice soothed the fears so that eventually Cox was able to sound "very vigorous and determined," delivering fiery, fist-thumping orations.[28]

When Cox began his service in the 61st Congress in 1908, his language supported Democratic causes of the day, including low tariffs. Cox said he believed American industry, including the many manufacturing plants around Dayton, had matured. One of his early speeches on the House floor favored free trade in coffee, tea, boots, shoes and hides, lumber, and zinc.[29] Many of his proposed bills supported pensions for residents of the Soldiers and Sailors Home near Dayton, which Cox recognized as a Republican stronghold that he could turn. His other presentations favored Progressive themes, including the populist drives for

Good Roads 21

grassroots initiative and referendum—two methods by which citizens could prompt legislation—and a national income tax. "I am a Progressive," Cox said. "I should make it clear that my own allegiance from the start had been with the progressive wing of the Democratic Party."[30]

Cox also remained actively associated with his newspapers, writing editorials and keeping an eye on management during his years in Washington. The continued business association assured "organs which I could place behind the new progressive ideas of the day," he said,[31] but the connection to Dayton didn't extend to his personal life. One contemporary observer noted Cox had "practically no outside interests" and that he did not join other patricians playing golf. At a stocky 170 pounds on a 5'6" frame, he preferred instead to camp in the Canadian woods to swim and fish for a couple of weeks with his oldest son, James.[32] Numerous photographs in his Washington living quarters, as well as frequent mentions of the Cox children in casual conversation, illustrated Cox's devotion to his sons James and John and daughter Helen, and he attempted to assure the family's well-being back home. They lived comfortably just north of downtown Dayton in a Cox-built Queen Anne-style mansion, but Cox and his wife Mayme couldn't make the magnificent house a loving home during his years in Congress. Mayme and the children didn't accompany him to the nation's capital, and in 1909 Mayme Simpson Cox moved out of the mansion in order to live in Cleveland; the couple formally divorced in June 1911. Cox arranged investments to support the children and never openly discussed the case or his relationship with Mayme.

Cox easily won a second term in Congress in 1910. Meanwhile his name was being whispered as potential for the Ohio governor's seat, a movement he did not discourage. The gubernatorial incumbent, Democrat Judson Harmon, had won the previous two-year term in the governor's seat against the fragmented Republican Party, but Harmon, a Cincinnati lawyer Cox knew from his days as an *Enquirer* reporter, espoused insufficiently progressive views that were, as Cox commented, "not in step with all of the elements creating the swift, progressive pace that was then on." Nevertheless, Harmon called for the statewide constitutional convention that offered a large slate of reforms to counteract what Cox described as "reactionary" state government. Ohio's voters accepted most of the reforms in the special election of September 1912, approving thirty-four of forty-two proposed constitutional revisions; only women's suf-frage issues failed. The reforms empowered citizens through initiative and referendum laws, created line-item vetoes for the governor, reorga-nized the state judicial system, and created a statewide civil service program. The changes, Cox said, "gave Ohio what was generally regarded as one of the most liberal of all state constitutions."[33]

Concurrently the state's Democrats met and by acclamation approved Cox as their candidate for governor. Cox campaigned as an unabashed Progressive, fixing his name to support for the liberal reforms beyond those of the state constitutional convention. He had already spoken in Congress in favor of laws opposing child labor and supported the use of convict labor in road improvement projects. In the summer of 1912 he toured forty Ohio counties to assert support for a woman's right to hold office, the direct election of US senators, a system of home rule for local-ities, an eight-hour workday on public works, changes in the judicial system, prison reform, and improvement of roads and highways in Ohio.

In the general election that November, Cox triumphed easily over the Republican and Bull Moose candidates, and the new governor immedi-ately set about cementing a Progressive agenda. In his first speech to the Ohio general assembly Cox expressed support for improved roads through increased sale of state bonds and prison reform that included a new penitentiary and a system of paying prison workers a small wage.[34] In 1913 he named a new Ohio State Penitentiary warden, forty-two-year-old Preston Elmer Thomas, a former teacher in the Wapakoneta, Ohio, school district who had moved into the position of a prison parole officer. The governor told Thomas he wanted "the best prison in the world."[35]

At the same time, federal money stimulated work on Ohio's rural roads. The number of motor vehicle registrations nationally had risen from about eight thousand at the turn of the century to a half million a decade later,[36] and the new motorists, along with the bicyclists, put con-stant pressure on Congress. "Congressmen began introducing good-roads bills in Congress, and in the first decade of the new century there seemed to be almost as many road building schemes as congressmen," historian Wayne Fuller wrote.[37]

On a national level, a trend toward a more sophisticated highway system easily fit into the new administration of the Republican President,

Good Roads 23

William Howard Taft, who had defeated Progressive Democrat William Jennings Bryan in the 1908 presidential election. Taft, an Ohioan like Douglas and Cox, was himself fascinated by automobiles, which his predecessor Theodore Roosevelt called "devil wagons." Three of Taft's machines now filled White House spaces that had recently sheltered presidential horses.[38]

To mollify the Better Roads Movement, Taft pushed Congress to appropriate $500,000 as a seed fund to help local governments study new road-building techniques. Under the Taft plan, the federal government would distribute $10,000 to each state for research into improved local roads, with the proviso that the spending be controlled by experts in the federal Office of Road Inquiry, renamed as the Office of Public Roads.

Before the money could be allocated, however, bitter dissension between Roosevelt's Bull Moose Party and Taft Republicans ousted the Taft administration. Progressive Democrat Woodrow Wilson reaped the benefits of the congested three-way presidential contest of 1912, and after he took over the US presidency, one of Wilson's early priorities was to reorganize the half-million-dollar allocation for roads. The $10,000 spending limit was abandoned, and the new administration chose instead to find projects that would test road-building methods in a variety of climates.

As one of its initial experiments, the Office of Public Roads chose to upgrade about twenty-four miles of the National Road in Ohio, from near Newark east to Zanesville. Although historian Fuller suggested sentiment motivated a desire to recover the famous old Pike,[39] the National Road had become a narrow, muddy, and rutted path that needed to be completely repaved. Government plans called for the most economical surface, which federal experts found to be new concrete paving methods. Unfortunately, this scientific opinion didn't sit well in southeast Ohio: "As it happened, over a thousand men were employed in the Zanesville brick factories, and the revelation of the government's decision to use cement on the road threw the Zanesville Chamber of Commerce in a tizzy," historian Fuller reported.[40] Brick company executive Rufus C. Burton fumed that no option other than brick paving would be allowed. The local governments appealed to Governor Cox and State Highway Commissioner James R. Marker, who carried the argument to the federal government, to no avail. It would be cost-saving concrete or nothing. When it was sug-

A cartoon illustrating the conflict between various types of paving available to National Road contractors. Better Roads and Streets *magazine, 1916*

gested the entire federal appropriation for the Ohio roads project might be moved to another state, local forces retreated: the National Road from Newark to Zanesville was paved with concrete.[41]

The active participation of the governor, combined with matching state funds that accompanied the project, allowed the Cox plan for Progressive reform to continue in Ohio. "Prior to this, the building of highways was influenced by politics," Cox said. "In many of our counties you could easily locate the county commissioners because they lived on good roads."[42] In addition, Cox complained that the state's hundreds of small public school districts had evolved into local fiefdoms rife with patronage, a memory he drew upon from his youth. "These two improvements supplemented each other," Cox wrote, "for in the consolidation of [school]

Good Roads

districts and the running of school buses, better roads were highly necessary."[43] Money for better roads throughout the state, and the state portion of the National Road project, came as part of funding legislation called the Hite Law. Opponents called it a government intrusion into local politics and bitterly contested the bill.

Cox unabashedly fought back. In 1913, at his first address to the state legislature, he called for a law improving roads as part of a general reform movement that also included a request to allow use of prison labor in state road projects. Cox turned quickly to Ohio's county commissioners, asking them at their statewide meeting in early 1913 to "be liberal in road appropriations."[44] Then he shepherded a half-mill tax levy for road construction through the state legislature, where opponents battled the tax legislation all the way to the Ohio Supreme Court. The tax levy passed muster and brought so much income to the state that Cox had it reduced by half the following year.

With substantial funds in place, Ohio and local counties were able to equal a federal government allotment of $140,000 for the National Road project. Bonds sold in Newark, the county seat of Licking County, and Zanesville, the county seat of Muskingum County, matched the Washington dollars on a local level, while the state of Ohio kicked in another $80,000 in order to extend the project in a westward direction, from Newark to the Franklin County line outside of Columbus. Groundbreaking for the project was scheduled for the spring of 1914.

But reactionary forces couldn't swallow the new Progressive agenda. Cox and his supporters were called socialists, and when Cox instigated his program to tie wholesale school modernization to a system of highways and market roads, conservatives hauled out spokespeople who testified for the traditional one-room schoolhouses and lifestyle of old. Cox paraphrased one opponent who spoke at a public meeting: "I don't like these newfangled notions," the man said. "The little red brick schoolhouse was good enough for Pap, it was good enough for me and it is good enough for my children."[45]

Republicans amassed other forces against Cox. The governor's support for workmen's compensation reform motivated the insurance industry, and in the months approaching the 1914 elections Cox observed an anti-Catholic movement promoted by literature and slogans published throughout the state. This affected the Senate race between Democrat Timothy Hogan, a Roman Catholic, and Republican Warren G. Harding. "Early in the campaign it became apparent that a great fanaticism was developing," Cox observed,[46] so to show his opposition to the anti-Catholic movement he campaigned with Hogan. At the same time, the question of alcohol prohibition moved into the public consciousness, fed by new Ohio laws that limited the number of alcohol-sales licenses. Democratic supporters urged Cox to withhold the names of people who had received licenses, but Cox refused to hide the list in an effort to keep politics out of the issue, while gubernatorial candidate Frank B. Willis, a prohibitionist, took advantage of the conflict to drive a wedge between wet and dry proponents.

Ultimately Willis won a close 1914 governor's election, with the Democratic vote split between Cox and James R. Garfield, the Progressive Party candidate and son of the twentieth president. Cox called Willis the child of the prohibitionist Anti-Saloon League, and described him as "a jovial fellow, big in heart and body, the kind that never took public service very seriously." Apparently the new governor's inattention mollified conservative angst. In the case of the Newark-Zanesville National Road project, for example, the Willis administration froze state funding, saying construction could not proceed without ready state cash. This action dismayed the local governments in Licking and Muskingum counties, which had sold bonds providing two-thirds of the total cost of the road construction. They quickly appealed to Willis, who relented and allowed contracts to be let so the work proceed.

III

War Roads

BETWEEN 1914 AND 1916 James M. Cox hunkered in his Dayton newspaper office like a coiled spring, watching the Willis administration's unsuccessful efforts to dismantle reform. In the summer of 1916 Cox was renominated for gubernatorial candidate, and he observed that although the Republican Party had promised "things they had reviled would, of course be repealed," the reforms still stood after two years. That November Woodrow Wilson won a second term in the national election for president, and in Ohio Cox was elected for his second term as governor. His reforms now vindicated, he said later that "we called for no more major legislation." "The reform in all its major essentials had been complete."[1] The lame duck session of the state legislature retired in March without fanfare, but history would fill the Cox legislative agenda shortly: "The war fell upon us a month after the legislature adjourned," he recalled, "and quite naturally [we] were directed to support the federal government."[2]

President Wilson had tread cautiously around US entry into World War I, but he revised his plan of action when Germany tried to align with Mexico against the US and then renewed unrestricted submarine warfare in March 1917. Eighteen days after Congress approved Wilson's April 6 request to declare war, Raymond Beck, a rubber industry executive and one of the country's original roads experts, joined a group of business leaders in the expansive Columbus Statehouse office of Ohio Governor Cox. With a bust of nineteenth-century governor Salmon P. Chase looking over his shoulder, Beck shifted his large frame in a chair at the oval meeting table next to W. A. Alsdorf, president of the Ohio Good Roads Federation, George Lattimer of the Columbus Chamber of Commerce, and trucker S. M. Williams. The motoring advocates had gathered to warn Cox that railroads and interurbans wouldn't be able to carry the enormous amount of war matériel expected to cross Ohio. The answer, they said, would have to be mobilization of motor trucks, operating on Ohio roads.[3]

Their warning was neither novel nor unexpected. Since his days in the US Congress, Cox had advocated improved roadways in the state, linking their creation to progress in industry, agriculture, and education. The federal government in Washington, too, had been jolted by the Good Roads movement: the Office of Public Roads (OPR), headed by engineering expert Logan W. Page, became a Progressive exemplar. It fashioned, then administered, the Federal Aid Road Act of 1916, which promised to bring commerce to rural people on modern, efficient roads. The federal government would match state road funding up to $10,000 per mile on road construction projects. The money was to be distributed through the highway departments of the individual states because the road support experiment of 1912 had taught the OPR to overlook local governments and to insist on the Progressive hallmark of efficient administration of highway projects.[4]

Beck, representing the rubber tire industry, possessed fundamental knowledge about roads. In his youth in New Jersey at the turn of the century, he motored throughout the Northeast, taking note of the muddy trails, gravel paths, and paved routes in order to produce some of the earliest road maps in the country. Beck published many of his tours in 1911 as *The Scenic New England Tour Book* while working as a freelance cartographer for the Automobile Club of America and other nascent motoring groups. It is likely that his maps provided directions for Congressman Albert Douglas and his wife during their daring 1910 motor tour from Washington, DC, through New England to upstate New York, then to Cleveland and home to Chillicothe.

In 1912 the B. F. Goodrich Rubber Company of Akron, Ohio, discovered Beck's expertise and hired him as director of its new Goodrich Touring Bureau. Goodrich, recognizing a need to encourage new motorists to use its products, had been sending a two-person crew into the coun-

Raymond Beck. The Ohio Motorist 13, vol. 1 (February 1921), 10

tryside to erect road signs and direction markers, but it soon understood the potential extent of the task. Beck had been making maps under his own name for years, and "from these maps and records we compiled right off the bat some of our earlier touring literature," recalled E. C. Tibbetts, the first head of the Bureau. "That literature was compiled absolutely independent of any road checking operations of our own because it was his."[5]

Under Beck, the Goodrich Touring Bureau office staff grew to comprise Beck, two map makers, two typists, and a clerk who gathered and filled requests for touring information. On the road, the company fielded three White Motor Company trucks with a crew of two in each, and two motorcyclists who logged and measured the routes to be mapped. Beck himself traveled frequently, representing Goodrich and serving on several boards that advocated good roads. The freedom of the road seemed to suit him, as illustrated in Goodrich company literature where Beck had gushed that motor touring was "the ultimate elixir of life." Tibbetts further painted the picture: "Beck was, in many respects, just a big, overgrown boy," he said. "[Beck] was a fellow who never worried, and whether a thing was going good, bad, or indifferent, responsibility in the strict meaning of the word meant little or nothing to him."[6] Others chided his large size as well: as an Akron Chamber of Commerce group prepared to attend a convention, one observer said their colleague Beck would "have to pick out an extra-long berth."[7]

Regardless of his casual demeanor, Beck became ubiquitous for the Touring Bureau as a promoter of good roads. In June 1913, he predicted an interstate highway connecting New York and Chicago via Akron.[8] In December 1913, as a member of the Chamber of Commerce Good Roads Committee, he co-signed an open letter to the Summit County commission, urging improvement of roads throughout the county surrounding Akron.[9] In October 1914, in a letter to the editor published in the *Akron Beacon Journal*, Beck urged paving of all roads around Akron. "A brick road is unquestionably the logical road for the main-market highways," he wrote, "but our entire attention should not be given to these roads alone."[10] At the beginning of 1917, he was named a director and roads chairman of the Akron Automobile Club, and in February, as the states prepared to receive the funds from the 1916 Federal Aid Road Act and war clouds darkened the horizon, he anticipated the strategic importance of roads: "Akron's rubber factories, isolated as they are by stretches of mud on all sides, and hampered by freight congestion on the railroads, would be helpless in case of national peril," he said as a representative of the Ohio Good Roads Federation.[11] In March 1917, Beck had to intervene as roads chairman of the Akron Auto Club in favor of the increasing commerce involving big rigs. A trucker en route from Cleveland to Akron refused to yield half the roadway, so the auto driven by Grover Reese, secretary of the Auto Club and a proponent of higher speed limits, could squeeze past. When he finally was able to pass, the incensed Reese raced ahead to acquire a warrant from a local justice of the peace, who had the truck driver, Tony Raymond, stopped and fined $5. Reese then declared he would repeat the stunt in order to "break up the custom of truck drivers of hogging the highway," but Beck stepped in. "The truck is here to stay and has demonstrated its usefulness in interurban freight hauling," he said. "The club will, however, go after drivers who refuse to give up half the road.... We have notified employers to caution their men."[12]

The importance of truck transport quickly became apparent when war was declared. The nation's railroads, mired in financial difficulties even before the US entered the war, proved increasingly unable to ferry enough men and machines to embarkation points on the East Coast. "The [rail]roads were already so crowded by what the Allies had done in purchasing war supplies that a great deal of confusion had resulted," reported contemporary war chronicler Francis March. "The Allies had expended more than three billion dollars in the United States, and as nearly all of their purchases had to be sent to a few definite points for shipment to Europe, the congestion at those points had become a serious difficulty."[13] The railroads hastily assembled a wartime governing board, but while executives dickered, rail cars sat fully loaded at the docks and out of service until they could be emptied.

Beck and the motoring executives had predicted this transportation disaster in their April 1917 meeting with Governor Cox, but the nation's highways were hardly ready to support motor trucks hauling heavy loads of war matériel. A 1914 survey conducted by the federal Office of Public Roads found that out of more than two million miles of roads in the nation, only thirty-two thousand miles had been paved;[14] outside of cities, most American roads remained gravel or dirt. Roads were so bad that army trucks manufactured in the Midwest had to be hauled on rail cars to the East Coast ports, where they sat amid lines of loaded cars extending one hundred miles outside of the New York City.[15] Moreover, Midwest contractors, chambers of commerce, and auto manufacturers howled when Secretary of War Newton Baker issued a letter in late April 1917 requesting a moratorium on construction and maintenance of all but major highways on the coasts and around the Great Lakes.[16] With more than five million motor vehicles on the nation's roads, motoring had become a way of life in the US, said *Better Roads and Streets* magazine, adding, "Why we should discontinue the construction of our roads in these critical times, is beyond the comprehension of the average thinking citizen."[17] The United States Chamber of Commerce, worried that the country's war footing would set aside hard-won road improvement projects, met in a war convention in the summer of 1917 and resolved that "prompt and continued improvement of public highways should be the order of the day." Beck, from his post as Roads Committee Chairman of the Ohio Chamber of Commerce, added, "The action of the [Chamber's] war convention . . . is very encouraging to the road enthusiasts of the

United States."[18] At the same time, the Ohio Good Roads Federation sought and received assurances from the Cox administration that road building and repair would not be disrupted by the war.

The federal government soon realized it had to do something about the complaints arising from its draconian proposals. Use of Beck's unique experience became part of its response: in an effort to determine the actual sorry state of the nation's roads and highways, the War Department in May 1917 "borrowed" Beck from Goodrich. His task, according to the Secretary of War Newton Baker, was to count and evaluate roads between the Mississippi River and the Eastern seaboard in anticipation of military use.[19] A few months later, the US Council of National Defense, an executive war-preparedness group appointed by President Wilson in 1916, created a Highways Transport Committee. Hudson Motor Car Company president Roy W. Chapin headed the group, which included Logan W. Page, director of the Office of Public Roads. Beck was assigned to the committee as Chief Field Engineer.

The nation's trucking industries recognized the opportunity. They allied themselves with the national chamber of commerce and various auto clubs to lobby for representation on the Highways Transport Committee and for use of motor transport on improved highways. To further illustrate the utility of trucks, manufacturers in Toledo and Akron devised a plan with the Office of Public Roads, the US Army, and the Ohio Highway Department to drive newly minted trucks from assembly points in Akron and Toledo, Ohio, to the East Coast. The trucks were routed mostly over the Lincoln Highway, a transcontinental assemblage of paved main roads that took them through northern Ohio and Pennsylvania. The first trucks left Toledo in December 1917, and although within days the convoy encountered a blizzard, the truckers proved the concept of actually driving big trucks to embarkation points. After struggling through ice and snow in Pennsylvania's Allegheny Mountains for three weeks, twenty-nine of the thirty trucks reached the East Coast.

Uplifted by news on January 4 that the convoy had arrived in Baltimore, motor truck industry representatives met in New York the second week of January. To get more trucks on more highways, they planned with the government's Highways Transport Committee to send out a "pathfinder" vehicle, under the direction of Beck, tasked with finding routes

War Roads

that could feed from factories into the nation's two most significant east–west arteries, the National Road and the Lincoln Highway.

The pathfinder car, a seven-passenger Hudson Super-Six from Committee Chairman Chapin's factory, left the B. F. Goodrich plant in Pittsburgh the first week of March 1918, no doubt driven by Beck and carrying Major W. D. Uhler of the Quartermaster's Department, Captain C. B. Butchers of the Engineers Corps, and road engineers from Pennsylvania and Ohio. The plan was for the group to meet highway department representatives in Wisconsin, Illinois, Michigan, Indiana, and Ohio in order to identify the best, or potentially best, routes for about forty thousand three-ton trucks that the military had purchased and planned to move under their own power to the East Coast.[20]

The search confirmed what Rep. Albert Douglas had observed seven years earlier and what Beck had predicted: in Ohio, the big Hudson trundled over wildly inconsistent surfaces on the National Road, supposedly one of two major highways the military would use. Beck found one stretch of about twenty-five miles between Zanesville and Old Washington in eastern Ohio particularly appalling. During the bitter winter, coal trucks, with their solid, hard-rubber tires, had chewed up the Pike and areas bordering it so much that the trucks, even when empty, steered off the road onto adjoining yards, to the dismay of property owners. In a newspaper article topped by a headline stating that the National Road "Has the Appearance of Being Shelled by Huns," officials of the city of Cambridge called the Pike "impassible."[21]

Beck contacted Governor Cox and arrived at the Ohio Statehouse early the morning of March 12. It had been a year since he and Cox had last met, and this time, as a representative of the National Council of Defense, Beck had more than a warning. He told the governor that if Ohio was to help the war effort, the National Road would have to be upgraded across the state and totally rebuilt in southeast Ohio from Zanesville to Old Washington. Cox readily agreed to meet the challenge. His enthusiasm, however, would expose both positive and negative aspects of the Progressive Movement.

IV

Forty Thousand Trucks

GOVERNOR COX WASTED no time when he heard Beck's assessment of the National Road problem in Ohio. He immediately called together State Highway Commission Chairman A. R. McCulloch, State Auditor A. Victor Donahey, and Ohio Attorney General Joseph McGhee to formulate the state's approach to the federal government's stern message. Contemporary biographer Charles Morris described Cox as "a man of quick decision [and] a tendency to suddenness.... He is willing to tackle problems before others would seize hold of them."[1] In less than two hours Cox determined to declare the roads situation a war emergency. Next, he arranged for the state officials to gather later that day with representatives of Muskingum County in Zanesville, a city of about thirty thousand and the county seat, situated on the Pike some fifty-six miles from Columbus.

County and city officials in those eastern Ohio communities greeted news of the impending visit of the governor and his entourage with open arms. "The announcement that the National Pike improvement has been declared a war emergency by the government will be read with joy in Zanesville, Muskingum County and southeastern Ohio," the Zanesville *Signal* reported on its front page that afternoon. "It means this city and county will be on the main traffic line for government transportation, and that hundreds of trucks bearing materials for government and war use will pass through this city weekly.

Forty Thousand Trucks   35

"It will also provide this city with as excellent shipping facilities east as the improvement of the pike west has done in that direction."[2]

The Cox party left Columbus around noon Tuesday, March 12, making good time on the portion of the National Road that had been renovated with cement paving between 1914 and 1915. The travel party arrived in Zanesville about four p.m., and the governor must have found their destination delightful: the Clarendon Hotel at Fourth and Main Streets, across the street from the Muskingum County Courthouse in the heart of the city, featured eighty-eight rooms in a four-story brick edifice of Italianate-influenced architectural style and a restaurant of good repute. It advertised itself as "Ohio's Famous Hotel," and "Strictly First Class," and best of all, it had a large cigar shop just inside the hotel's broad double-door entrance, where Cox could pick up a few fine cigars or perhaps even a plug of chewing tobacco, one of his private pleasures.[3]

At six p.m. Cox, Auditor of State Donahey, Attorney General McGhee, Highway Commissioner Cowen, Council of National Defense Engineer Beck, and three members of the State Highway Advisory Board met across the street in the county auditor's office with the Muskingum County commissioners and prosecuting attorney. The additional presence of Rufus C. Burton of the Burton-Townsend Brick Company and Ohio State Penitentiary Warden Preston Elmer Thomas hinted at construction strategy for the project. Cox spoke first to outline the purpose of the unique gathering, then invited Beck to explain why the government had classified the reconstruction of the National Road as urgent. Beck said the military expected shortly to move forty thousand trucks from Midwest manufacturing plants through Ohio to the Atlantic Coast, but the condition of the National Road in southeast Ohio at the time made that impossible. The Pike from Zanesville east for more than twenty-five miles would have to be rebuilt.

Cox then turned to Burton. The contractor who insisted on brick pavement in 1914 had already signed a $469,000 agreement with Muskingum County to continue to renew the National Road after the brief hiatus during the Willis administration. The governor asked if Burton would accept declaration of the project as a war emergency, forcing the contractor to speed up his work.

Rufus C. Burton of the Zanesville, Ohio, Burton-Townsend Brick Company. Burton was the head contractor for the Muskingum County portion of the National Road work. The Clay Worker *magazine, February 1921, 142*

"Whatever you want done, whatever you want me to do, I'm at your service," he was heard to reply over applause.[4]

County officials followed with assurances to Cox that they had their share of money for the rebuilding project "in hard cash," by which they meant $294,000 acquired through the sale of construction bonds (about $5 million in today's dollars). They discussed with Attorney General McGhee the care needed to create a funding system that incorporated the money from the local bonds, a 50 percent federal government match, and state appropriations that would make up the remainder of costs. Burton was asked to meet quickly with subcontractors to plan the project and begin grading, and as co-owner of one of the area's largest brick-making plants, he was also able to assure the group that millions of paving bricks were available immediately. No one brought up the topic of concrete, the less-expensive material used just two years previously to pave the National Road from Columbus to Zanesville.

The following morning Cox and his traveling group bounced east across about twenty miles of unimproved Pike to Cambridge, the county seat of Guernsey County. In a festive atmosphere that repeated the Zanesville agenda, a representative from the state attorney general's office followed the governor's address with a discussion of the legal aspects of using prisoner labor and promised to draw up a resolution of approval for consideration by the Guernsey County commissioners.

Cox and his administrators were compelled to employ such persuasion because the National Road project's proposed use of convict labor in Guernsey County skirted the edge of Ohio law. The state's constitution, copying the US Constitution's 13th Amendment, outlawed slavery and involuntary servitude in Ohio, "unless for the punishment for crime." As elsewhere in the nation, Ohio prison administrations always had preferred hard labor over idle confinement, but reformers in the Progressive Era added the requirement that those who were incarcerated be both rehabilitated and educated. Beginning with the first meeting of the American Congress of Corrections in Cincinnati in 1870, prison reformers began to encourage prison-education curricula and indeterminate sentencing, through which rehabilitated convicts were granted early release. In the late nineteenth-century New York's Elmira Reformatory, under leadership of warden Zebulon Brockway, initiated reform programs that included work projects designed to transform inmates into working-class citizens.[5] At New York's Sing Sing Correctional Facility, reformer Thomas Mott Osborne installed a series of reforms from the last decade of the nineteenth century until well into the twentieth century. "Outside the walls a man must choose between work and idleness,—between honesty and crime," Mott said in a 1904 address to the National Prison Association. "Why not let him teach himself these lessons before he comes out?"[6] In Ohio, Superintendent Thomas C. Jenkins of the Ohio State Reformatory in Mansfield, which opened in 1896, repeatedly described its role as reform, not punishment, with classes offered in basic instruction such as reading and writing as well as trades.[7]

James M. Cox had a long history of advocating for prison reform and use of prison labor on highway projects, which he called "a humane affair."[8] Campaign biographer Morris, in his contemporary review of the Cox governorship, observed, "Prisoners now earn their freedom through work in the healthful out-of-doors on highways, in plants for making road material, and on farms. There is a system of compensation to the families for work done as a balance on which to begin life anew."[9] Outside of Ohio, similar sentiments about using convict labor for highway projects were expressed in a November 1917 editorial in *Good Roads* magazine. In the July 1917 issue of *Better Roads and Streets* magazine, S. M. Williams of the Garford Motor Truck Company described beneficial prison labor systems in highway projects across the country, although he acknowledged they were unpopular with the general public and organized labor.[10]

Both magazines explained that the public distrusted prison labor because of how it was fashioned. Programs that used convicts as laborers took one of three forms: the contract system, under which prisoners were farmed out to private contractors who profited from the free labor, as for example in chain gangs of the South; the state account system, under which the state alone operated profitable prison industries that provided goods on the open market; and the state use system, under which contractors or firms utilized prison labor that generally remained under state supervision.[11] In Ohio, forces of private commerce and organized labor, alarmed at the prospect of low-cost labor undercutting markets, teamed in 1906 to pass House Bill 77, commonly known as the Wertz Law, which outlawed contract labor in Ohio and established a state use system. Eventually prisoners manufactured their own soap, clothing, and shoes, while producing furniture, printing, and basic iron and sheet metal work such as road signs and auto tags.

A state-owned brick plant in southeast Ohio, which nominally manufactured paving bricks for state highway construction, also used state prison labor. The plant was unable to provide nearly enough bricks for the Muskingum and Guernsey County projects, but it provided the entry for Cox to use convicts in the National Road highway construction because the plant created a ready-made source of experienced labor. Its employees hadn't been chosen at random for the backbreaking work, but through "scientific" methods adopted by the Ohio prison administration.

Such an approach fundamentally introduced racial bias into official policies, including those used to make prison labor personnel decisions. Language in the contemporary *Annual Report of the Ohio Board of Administration to Governor Cox*, which proudly outlined Ohio's state use system of prison labor, clearly illustrates the situation in the days when Black recruits were being gathered for the National Road project:

> We believe that the fundamental idea is service to the State. To do away with idleness and to instill habits of industry and thrift is not only good religion, but good business.
>
> ... We operate a brick plant about forty-two miles southeast of Columbus and employ from eighty to a hundred prisoners. ... These men not only quarry the shale, but operate the machinery, load the kilns and do

Forty Thousand Trucks

all of the work required. We were able to select a certain number of prisoners who had experience in this kind of work, and the industry is one we believe that is best adapted to this class of labor, and particularly the colored element, as it is an industry that does not require men of large mental caliber, but what we designate as "strong back" men, the operations being largely manual.[12]

This application of human typology that incorporated racial stereotyping utilized the recognized science of the time. For example, in 1887, before authorities in Ohio prisons accepted fingerprinting, they adopted the Bertillon system of prisoner identification. Under this system, innovative at the time, prison operatives photographed, physically measured, and categorized each prisoner according to racial characteristics, physical attributes, and social background. Devised in France by the eccentric anthropologist Alphonse Bertillon, the method created card files that could be meticulously organized and interrogated. The efficiency of this method attracted Progressives.

Thus the *Annual Report of the Ohio Board of Administration* raised no eyebrows when it landed on the desk of Governor Cox, because what is today seen as obvious racism would have been considered merely Progressive efficiency. Although modern scholars argue that application of true Progressive Movement thought dates from the 1890s to about 1920, whereas racism purported to be based on scientific principles long predates the Progressive Movement,[13] unquestioning Progressives frequently absorbed and applied pre-Civil War traditions and theories of race.

These traditions had grown out of white European culture steeped in supposed superiority. Ethnic Studies scholar Ronald Takaki observes, for example, that in Shakespeare's *The Tempest*, written in 1611, the exiled duke Prospero enslaves a non-white island native for labor that enriches Prospero.[14] Before the American Revolution, Arthur Lee of Virginia wrote that Black people and Native Americans should be separated from whites because they were uncivilized and therefore not rational.[15] The First Congress of the United States enacted the Naturalization Act of 1790, under which the new nation could filter out undesirable people seeking entry into the country while allowing free white person[s] "of good character."[16]

Concepts of racial superiority took on an air of science following the 1859 publication of Charles Darwin's *Origin of Species*. Stirred by the eighteenth-century writing of Thomas Malthus, who postulated that only the strongest members in any environment survive because population outstrips food supply, Darwin developed his theory of the evolution of species during his famous voyage to the South Seas aboard the HMS *Beagle*. Organisms evolve from common ancestors in a slow, continuous process, Darwin said; he offered no comment regarding topics of race.

Debate expanded quickly beyond Darwin, however. While Darwin fled the controversy that his work had initiated and became a virtual recluse, his friend Thomas Huxley expanded the theory by suggesting a monogenist approach under which humans evolved from a single stem. Huxley's former mentor, the German Rudolph Virchow, suggested a polygenist theory in which various races of humankind arose separately. Virchow could not bring himself to accept Darwin's theory, but his fellow German and bitter rival Ernst Haeckel enthusiastically endorsed the proposition that humans evolved from lower creatures. Haeckel and his acolytes twisted evolutionary theory far beyond Darwin—paleoanthropologist Pat Shipman explains:

> A distorted concept of human race was at the heart of Haeckel's theories.... To Haeckel, a race was a nationality, a tribe or even an ethnic group who differed culturally but not genetically from their neighbors. Another race was 'them' to 'us'.... He flatly believed that races were as different from each other as species of animals, offering what seemed to be outright scientific support for racism. He reasoned that, because the "lower races such as the Veddahs [of India] or Australian Negroes [*sic*] are psychologically closer to mammals (apes and dogs) than to civilized Europeans, we must assign a totally different value to their lives."[17]

Thus bolstered by science, racial theory jumped the Atlantic Ocean in time to become a factor in post-Civil War Reconstruction. Yale economist Francis Amasa Walker, who in his life had been chief of the Federal Bureau of Statistics, commissioner of the Bureau of Indian Affairs, and president of Massachusetts Institute of Technology, claimed that science could be used to manage new technologies and control society. From his positions of influence, Walker said American genius grew from racial superiority and frontier experience of its white settlers, and as the nation grew across North America, he sought a homogeneous society. At the same time in

Forty Thousand Trucks

the post-rebellion American South, *Atlanta Constitution* editor Henry W. Grady, son of a Georgia merchant, called for a "New South" in which the Black population of former enslaved people became a working class separated from white society. For his contemporary, New Orleans author George Washington Cable, Black people in this New South were unbridled barbarians who needed the paternalism of the white population to give them the opportunity to increase their intellectual growth.

Measurement of the intellect became a scientific goal at the beginning of the twentieth century with the testing conducted by psychologists Robert Yerkes and Lewis Terman. Yerkes examined military recruits and determined that Polish and Black people scored poorly, although he neglected to account for factors such as illiteracy and English fluency. Terman developed his Stanford-Binet intelligence test in 1905 and used results from its application to suggest that leaders could steer workers toward employment that best matched their IQ scores.[18]

This research, supported by data that measured intelligence and physical characteristics, morphed into eugenics, the belief that the human population can be improved by removing "inferior" members. In Germany, the virulently anti-Semitic Haeckel founded the German Monist League in 1906, with the goal of purification of German society through the use of eugenics principles. In the United States, the Eugenics Records Office, founded in 1904 in New York with money from the Carnegie Institute, discouraged interracial marriage and supported sterilization of the "feeble-minded."[19] This concept received legal approval with the Supreme Court's 1927 case Buck v. Bell, which allowed sterilization of seventeen-year-old Carrie Bell after she gave birth to an illegitimate child who was judged intellectually inferior by the Eugenics Records Office.

The Progressive Movement in the United States coexisted with these concepts. President Woodrow Wilson, a Progressive, rose from a family that had served the Confederacy in Virginia to become a history scholar and president of Princeton University. In his 1902 work, *A History of the American People*, he expressed decidedly Southern views of Reconstruction after the Civil War, observing "the troubles in the southern States arose out of the exclusion of the better whites from the electoral suffrage no less than from the admission of the most ignorant blacks."[20] *[sic]* At the behest of several members of his presidential cabinet, Wilson's administration reversed desegregation practices in federal hiring. Although subsequent scholarship has attempted to soften Wilson's reputation, an article by Kathleen Wolgemuth in *The Journal of Negro History* noted that "Wilson did know about the plans for racial separation in the government. He approved of them. He vigorously defended the official policy of segregation in a series of personal letters."[21]

Ohio's progressive Democratic leader had conflicting attitudes toward race relations. "We are a composite people in the United States," said Governor James Cox in campaign literature. "The belief of students of government in years past that our democracy would not endure was based entirely upon the idea that we could not build a nation from the blood of many races...It is very important, particularly at this time when racial impulses and emotions have been stirred worldwide...that we make the utmost effort to prevent division along these lines."[22] Former *Dayton Daily News* editor Agnes McCarty Ash, who worked for Cox, recalls similar positive attitudes that her employer espoused. "I do believe he was progressive for the time, but not for now," she said in 2019.[23]

In Cox's time, race relations in the United States had reached a nadir. In 1915 President Wilson screened the innovative but racist pro-Ku Klux Klan film *Birth of a Nation* in the White House, prompting great outcry from the young National Association for the Advancement of Colored People and individual civil rights activists. The film was so controversial that Ohio Governor Willis outlawed it in the state, but Cox, who had spoken in favor of film censorship during his campaign for Willis's job, reversed the censorship order when he returned to the governor's chair, arguing for historical clarity regarding Reconstruction. "I arranged a meeting with Thomas Dixon, author of *The Clansman* from which the film had been made," Cox wrote in his autobiography. "I said I wanted our people to have a better understanding of the outrages of the carpetbag rule in the South; that the younger generation was not being informed by the history books, and that the cause of national unity would be promoted if the North knew the terrible days through which the South had lived."[24]

In another example of Ohio's racial confusion at the time, Cox responded to the state of war in the summer of 1917 by creating the Ohio Branch, Council of National Defense in order to organize the state's activities in industry, transportation, propaganda, and patriotism. During a

Forty Thousand Trucks

meeting to establish its priorities, the council discussed a need for labor relations policies during the period of labor shortage, although it stopped short of issuing an open invitation to potential laborers. The council approved industrialist Harvey Firestone's idea to use vagrants and draft dodgers for upkeep of the state's highways, but "Cox assured the Council that his office was watching closely the influx of Negroes into the state," historian Cebula reports from council minutes, "and [Council vice-chair Fred] Croxton spoke against recruiting blacks [*sic*] 'for fear that a million of them might come to Ohio.'"[25]

V

Five Million Bricks

THE "UNPRECEDENTED STEP of putting hundreds of penitentiary prisoners to work"[1] to solve the labor problem on the National Road project, along with the racial stereotyping used to recruit those workers, seems to have been a foregone conclusion. Within two days of the meetings in Zanesville and Cambridge, state highway department crews had deposited rough-hewn lumber to be used to build housing for prison laborers at a site near the work route just east of the village of Old Washington, about eight miles east of Cambridge in Guernsey County. Newspapers reported that contractor Harness Renick of Fayetteville would lead a crew to hurriedly assemble barracks similar to military training camps of the time, with the newspapers adding that a wire enclosure would "probably" surround the camp.[2]

By Thursday afternoon, March 14, State Highway Department Engineer W. C. Fawcett and Muskingum County Engineer Ralph Strait had issued a command that farmers remove fences and mailboxes from the National Pike path borders, as the improved road would be returned to its original eighty-foot right-of-way. Surveyors were on hand to stake out the new boundaries.

Meanwhile, an exuberant Cox returned to Columbus to proclaim his satisfaction with the plans. "Commissioners and other officials of both Muskingum and Guernsey Counties were quick to realize the importance from a war standpoint in having the road improved in their counties," he

Five Million Bricks 45

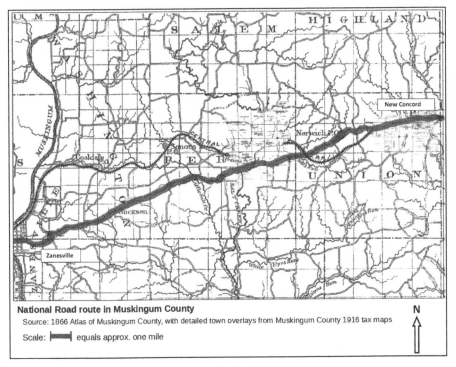

1866 Atlas of Muskingum County, with detailed town overlays from Muskingum County 1916 tax maps

said, adding that excavation would begin the following week, and prisoners would be transported to the work sites in Muskingum and Guernsey Counties.[3] Warden Preston Thomas of the Ohio State Penitentiary said in a statement that he would send a crew of fifty convicts, and that Mansfield Reformatory would send another fifty convicts.[4] A meeting with the governor Tuesday, March 19, would determine rates of reimbursement to the prison administration.[5] Renick, whose uncle William had invented an efficient, inexpensive method of paving with gravel, already had a road-building contract for Guernsey County. He asked for two hundred prisoners.

Warden Thomas said the first prisoner group would feature men who were eligible for parole or could be trusted and that they had expressed enthusiasm for an opportunity for outdoor work and a chance to help the war effort. He also noted that when the offer was announced, more prisoners stepped forward than he could use.

No records exist to hint at the veracity of the warden or the authenticity of the convicts' feelings. The prisoners did not hold Thomas in high esteem; they called him "the Pig," and his self-appointed vocation seems to have been to stop inmate escapes.[6] Although during his tenure as warden Thomas had established a prison trustee program and introduced indeterminate sentencing to allow early release of some convicts, author Mitchel Roth explained that "the warden's job was a juggling act between keeping inmates under control while exercising a modicum of diplomacy, an attribute that Warden Thomas was clearly deficient in."[7] Inmates accused Thomas of favoritism, and he held both prisoners and potential prison reformers in low regard. His methods could involve cruelty: the sight of men caged for minor violations and a wretched victim shackled to a wall in solitary confinement horrified one visiting lawyer. "I wondered whether this was really a civilized country in the second decade of the twentieth century," the visitor said.[8]

At the March 19 organizational meeting with the governor, the balloon of optimism deflated. Rufus Burton, of Zanesville's Burton-Townsend Brick Company, held the original contract of about $470,000 for restoration of the National Road in Muskingum County under the Willis administration. His firm had been offered a new contract for $154,316.55 to continue the job on one of the three sections in Muskingum County, but Burton declined to take the job. A Democrat well known to the Cox administration, Burton had volunteered in the Zanesville meeting to supervise the project for free, but now he said his company wouldn't do the work under the new guidelines that called for completion by July 1, 1918. "I feel it would be impossible for me to complete said contracts in accordance with the demands of the Federal Government...and I, therefore, write to you to notify you that I refuse to enter upon the completion of said contracts," he told the state attorney general's office. The Ohio Highway Department had little alternative but to accept his refusal, so its advisory board voted to return the project sections in Muskingum County to the state highway department. The work would be done "under contract, force account [direct payment for time and materials] or in such a manner as the State Highway Commissioner may deem for the best interest of the State of Ohio."[9]

Then the group—including Governor Cox, State Highway Commissioner Clinton Cowen and his advisory aides, Warden Thomas, Acting

Five Million Bricks   47

Superintendent Thomas C. Jenkins of Mansfield Reformatory, members of the state board of administration, and several contractors—decided that the state highway department could not run the operation in Muskingum County quickly enough. Instead, tasks would be doled out to seven subcontractors under Burton's charge. Bids for the work would be accepted until the end of the day Thursday, March 21, with winners announced that Friday, Burton told the newspapers. Contractors would be paid based on their actual costs plus a negotiated percentage, and they would employ labor from the communities; prison labor would not be used unless necessary.[10]

Plans remained unchanged for Guernsey County. Fifty prisoners were to be shipped there the following week, while construction of their living quarters continued apace. Another batch of convicts from the state penitentiary would follow, with more prison labor promised as needed.

"We expect this move to give a big boom for good roads in Ohio," Governor Cox announced after the meeting, "and we expect the contractors to play square and not imagine this is Christmas and the state of Ohio is playing Santa Claus."[11]

In a meeting the end of that week, the State Highway Board laid out just how "festive" the state was prepared to be. The Board agreed to pay Burton his actual costs plus a 20.5 percent fee for work completed and materials used up to July 1, declining monthly to a fee of 10 percent after October 1. This money would be used to pay laborers, teams of horses (including ten teams driven by Agnes Benz of Columbus and her crews), foremen, and superintendents.[12] According to the highway department, Burton was expected to continue this rate of pay through his subcontractors in Muskingum County.

But the federal government didn't take kindly to the state's plan to employ second-level subcontractors. In a letter to Highway Commissioner Cowen, H. K. Bishop, the district engineer of the federal Office of Public Roads, warned the highway department to avoid making a bunch of small contracts. "I would like to suggest that wherever possible in future [*sic*] the plan of asking for alternate bids be eliminated," he wrote, although the Feds were willing to be reasonable: "We realize, however, that there will be important local conditions which make such a plan impractical or inadvisable, and we do not want to insist on such a selection if the State Highway Department does not think it wise to make one."[13]

Horse-drawn "dragging," a first step in renovation on the National Road. The device pictured was derived from a split-log drag described in a 1908 US Department of Agriculture bulletin. It had been invented by Missouri farmer D. Ward King and was promoted by Office of Public Roads Director Logan W. Page. *ODOT construction photos collection, Ohio History Connection Archives, Series 2203 AV*

To illustrate the wisdom of the state's plan, the Highway Advisory Board invited the author of the letter, H. K. Bishop, to the next meeting of the board on the following Tuesday. In that gathering, the board outlined its desire to proceed with the Muskingum County work on a cost-plus-percentage basis and sought the federal government's formal approval. Bishop wanted assurances that the state could afford to finish the project, then made a long-distance phone call to Washington. Shortly thereafter a telegram arrived: "Satisfactory to let contract Ohio on cost plus basis. Wilson."

With permission granted from the highest level, the state began to assemble its forces. On Saturday, March 23, the Zanesville *Signal* included a front-page request that "every Zanesville and Muskingum County man who can do work on the East Pike and every Zanesville and Muskingum County man who has a team of horses which can be worked on the East Pike is being given the opportunity to 'do his bit.'" Contractor Burton, who up to now expressed no desire to use prison labor, asked men and teams to report for work Monday morning "to help win the war." At the

Five Million Bricks 49

Guernsey County 1916 township maps. *1916 Historical Atlas & Plats, Guernsey County Map Department, Guernsey County, Ohio*

same time, a steam shovel was rolled into place to begin grading the right-of-way between Zanesville and Cambridge.[14]

As if to confirm the urgency of the road-building project, Raymond Beck sent a telegram from the War Department announcing that within days the first of the new Liberty trucks would arrive on the National Road en route to Baltimore. He asked that the road east of Cambridge, at the time barely passable, be dragged to fill the ruts.[15]

The trucks, big seven-ton, open cab machines that trundled along at fifteen miles per hour maximum speed, did arrive, not in days but on May 9. Thirty trucks rolled into Cambridge after struggling for three hours on fifteen miles of unimproved Pike from Zanesville.

After the caravan parked along South Eighth Street in Cambridge, crews immediately set to cleaning and oiling the 425-cubic-inch, 52 hp engines. Cooks assembled a meal line behind the county jail, while a group of local women appeared with donated food. The following morning as the sun rose, Captain W. F. Walker, commander of the seventy-six men in the fleet, conferred with Ohio highway administrators and contractors and determined that continuing beyond Cambridge on the damaged National Road would be impossible.[16] The trucks and a second thirty-truck convoy following them turned north to intersect with the Lincoln Highway in order to complete the journey east.

Recognition that even sturdy army trucks couldn't navigate the old roadway testified to the depth of the task at hand. Despite Warden Thomas's optimistic statement on May 19 that he "hope[d] to celebrate the Fourth of July by riding over the completed National Highway,"[17] he couldn't keep his promise of sending the first assemblage of prison laborers to the Guernsey County part of the project the following Tuesday because Contractor Renick's crews hadn't finished the barracks near Old Washington. The western portion of the work site did have visitors that day, however: members of the State Highway Advisory Board, who joined Contractor Burton and state and county engineers in an inspection tour of the digging east of Zanesville, had moved on to kick dirt in Cambridge.

Four days later, fifty-nine convict laborers assembled at Union Station in Columbus for the short train ride to southeast Ohio. The men, all "colored," to use the language of the Columbus *Dispatch* report, wore civilian clothing and handcuffs and traveled under the supervision of three guards. The group detrained at Lore City, a hamlet southeast of Cambridge, and were transported to their new housing east of Old Washington.

Within days, contractors deemed their work in Guernsey County a great success. "I have heard all sorts of things about convict labor," said the crew's superintendent, Edgar Foy of Chillicothe, "and I never was more surprised in all my life than I have been by the way these men take hold." He guessed at the rate they were working that they would complete the 7.5-mile job in the county by early August.[18] In fact, the laborers outran their supplies: work slowed for several days while Renick negotiated with the state to allow purchase of local sand rather than wait for a shipment to be delivered. Nevertheless, the good roadway progress prompted contractors to arrange for more help, so a week later another fifty-five Black prisoners were assembled in the state penitentiary to hear a pep talk from the governor himself before they embarked on the trip east to National Road work.

"I went to the prison and talked to them," Cox recalled, "telling them it was their opportunity to render service to their country and that every man who labored industriously and behaved himself would have that fact registered in the prison."[19] In addition to hearing the governor's words, the men took an oath composed by Ohio Penitentiary clerk E. E. Stout,

Five Million Bricks 51

swearing with right hand raised to "faithfully perform your duty as honor men. By so doing, you will help preserve this great country in time of need and distress and each of you will help by doing your bit for the preservation of your government, civilization and liberty."[20]

Thus fortified, the prisoners rode into the open air of Guernsey County, where they were quickly put to work. About twenty miles west, in Muskingum County, supervisor Burton had declined at first to use convict labor; patriotic duty alone was supposed to be the motivation for the community laborers that Burton collected. The state provided plenty of supplies: it acquired sandstone for the road foundation at ten cents per ton, and then, at the request of federal engineer Beck, sought bids for crushed limestone. Burton's firm in Zanesville won the bid for up to five million paving bricks, at twenty-three cents per thousand; and the state purchased 5,600 barrels of concrete for curbs at $1.74 per barrel. But the stockpiles couldn't guarantee progress; in late April inspectors reported that Burton had not hired sufficient personnel and teams of horses for grading. Highway Commissioner Clinton Cowen complained to him in writing that if he didn't get moving on the project the state would "proceed to take such action as is necessary." A week later Burton sent a representative to the highway department advisory board asking the state to pay for the work under Burton's supervision at the time it was performed. The board refused Burton's request, stating that as stipulated in his contract, payment would be at completion of the project.

On May 7 Burton himself visited the Highway Advisory Board in Columbus. He explained that the work was behind schedule because half of April had been rainy (records show unusually low rainfall in April, although ten inches of snow fell in Muskingum County early in the month),[21] and besides, although he had plenty of laborers, he wasn't able to acquire enough teams of horses to accomplish much. He further complained that to complete the state's work he had found it necessary to rent an office and hire a receptionist, stenographer, and a bookkeeper (who happened to be his son-in-law) whom he paid $150 per month—about $30,000 annually in today's money. Burton asked the state to reimburse him for these costs, but the board made no decision.

Then Governor Cox stepped in. Clearly exasperated by the lack of progress on the construction project in Muskingum County, he called a meeting for May 17 in his office, where his private secretary, Charles E. Morris, represented him. State Auditor A. V. Donahey, Contractor Burton, and several of his sub-contractors crowded into the room, as did a battery of state officials including Highway Commissioner Clinton Cowen, members of the Highway Advisory Board, State Attorney General McGhee, special counsel John Kramer, Ohio Penitentiary Warden Thomas, and Mansfield Reformatory Acting Superintendent Jenkins.

Burton must have sunk in his seat as Donahey began the proceedings by reading a letter from Cox. In his message the governor warned that he had been following the lack of progress in Burton's section of the construction. Donahey added that he had heard rumors of cost overruns, so auditors would shortly present their report to the governor about them. Asked for an explanation of the situation, Burton reminded the state officials that although his subcontractors received the 20.5 percent fee for their work, he personally toiled gratis. Bad weather had complicated the work, he added, and the sixty-truck army caravan that just passed through had gouged the track.

Further, his subcontractors' efforts were inconsistent, he said, and he complained about the quality of his labor force. Advisory Board President McCulloch confirmed that he had visited the work site the previous week and found members of the construction crews standing idle or sitting around. He asked why the men weren't working; Burton said he didn't know.

Donahey conveyed the governor's suggestion that Burton accept two hundred convict laborers. Warden Thomas said he couldn't easily supply more workers, but Superintendent Jenkins of the Mansfield Reformatory offered to round up about one hundred young men from his institution, and possibly more. To discuss this offer Donahey, Cowen, and members of the advisory commission—but not Burton—reconvened in Donahey's office, where Cowen agreed that the highway department would pay for all expenses related to using Mansfield Reformatory laborers. They would be housed in a large circus-style tent, located along the National Road route between Zanesville and New Concord. The Highway Advisory Board formally approved this arrangement, and the board further agreed to a suggestion by Donahey to place a "competent accountant," as Governor Cox described the position, on the job in Muskingum County.[22]

Five Million Bricks 53

Rough stone is laid down between concrete curbs as an initial step in the paving process. Steam rollers would compact this layer, which would be covered by increasingly fine layers topped by bricks. *ODOT construction photos collection, Ohio History Connection Archives, Series 2203 AV*

Word of the Columbus meetings and possible cost overruns quickly reached southeast Ohio, alarming the Muskingum County administration. In a letter dispatched within days to Auditor Donahey, the county said it already was on the hook for $294,000—about $5 million in today's dollars—and it would pay no more for the National Road project in its county. Donahey hastily conferred with the governor, who responded immediately with a letter that Donahey read to the advisory board on May 21:

> "It is our judgment at the present time, as the result of a general change in the policy of administration in the construction work, that the funds now available will be sufficient," Cox wrote, adding that if more funding was needed he would go to the legislature to get it, a promise he would later regret. "We cannot afford to have the work suspended," he continued. "... At the outset we asked cooperation of your county, and it was given in the most splendid manner imaginable. I have no fault whatever to find with the action which you are taking for the protection of your county. I am convinced, however, that upon reflection you will not take any drastic step which would result in Muskingum County being directly responsible for any delay in the work."[23]

Now Cox turned his gaze to Guernsey County. In early June he called Contractor Renick, Warden Thomas, Highway Department Chief Cowen, and Advisory Board President McCulloch into his office for a progress report. Cox asked Renick when his section of the Pike would be completed, to which Renick replied on October 1. "That date will not do," Cox answered. "I expect the work to be completed prior to September 1." Could Renick finish the job if he had more prison help? Renick assured the governor that with additional help the work would be done on time.[24]

Cox turned to reliable Warden Thomas and received assurances that another fifty inmates could be found for Guernsey County work. Still not satisfied, Cox asked Cowen how many more convict laborers would help move along the Muskingum County portion of the project as well. "In my judgment, about another hundred," Cowen responded.

But Thomas and Cowen reminded the governor that increasing the number of convicts out in the field had its costs. In Guernsey County, Cowen said, conflict already had erupted between a state prison guard and construction supervisors, while in Muskingum County the single guard who kept watch over nearly a hundred reformatory prisoners had trouble keeping them busy. Without more guards, the state could expect "leakage" of men and equipment, Cowen warned.[25] He couldn't know that the state might plug the leaks of men and equipment, but it couldn't stop the clock.

VI

Sledgehammers and Picks

ACCORDING TO CONTEMPORARY newspaper reports, the convict laborers were "a happy, contented lot of men,"[1] "doing good work and happy in it,"[2] and satisfied to work "out in the open air and the sun away from penitentiary walls."[3] The newspapers claimed that the men recognized they were toiling in a patriotic project, and that the prison crews received a stipend, in a fashion. The highway department paid each prisoner $1.50 per day, but the money went to the prison administration to fund "expenses," which included the daily wage of sixteen cents actually paid to each convict. (Meanwhile, the Ferguson & Edmondson Company at the beginning of the summer paid its laborers thirty-one cents per hour.[4]) "The road commission is fortunate in getting its work done so cheap," commented the *Ohio State Journal* in its April 9 editorial.[5]

The prison laborers had a more ominous reason to be glad they were working outside of the Ohio State Penitentiary. Just as they left, the prison grapevine must have carried news that more than one hundred prisoners in the penitentiary had fallen ill with stomach pains and intestinal troubles. The prison doctor and consulting physicians concluded that their patients had been sickened by a jelly with an unusually bright color served at breakfast, which they determined to be contaminated. Administrators promised to stop distribution throughout the prison system, but within days the sickness affected more than five hundred penitentiary prisoners.

Dr. O. M. Kramer, the prison physician, eventually diagnosed the illness as influenza. He asked for the assistance of the state health department, which judged this flu to be extraordinarily contagious.[6] They were right: the prisoners had been infected in the early stages of an epidemic that came to be known as the Spanish flu, one of the great scourges of human history. Worldwide, it killed millions of victims, often young and previously vigorous.

The prisoners swinging picks and sledgehammers in the open air of Guernsey County got away just in time, because there were no reports of illness in their camp. In reality, both the Ohio Penitentiary convicts and later the Mansfield State Reformatory crews left overcrowded cells and highly orchestrated, disciplined, often cruel lifestyles to work in conditions very much like that of ordinary free laborers. The convict crews were emphatically not chain gangs: photos show that the prisoners wore civilian clothes and labored under the eyes of only a few unarmed guards. The Guernsey County convict workers from the Ohio Penitentiary slept in bedding supplied by the state in a rough wood dormitory similar to army barracks at Camp Sherman in nearby Chillicothe, Ohio, albeit more hastily constructed. By early May prison workers could retire at the end of the workday to the putt-putt of a four-horsepower pump drawing water from a large tank to showers in a bath building, a convenience no doubt appreciated by both attendants and laborers who returned from the field in perspiration-stained work clothes. In an adjacent wooden structure, the highway department fed the men, with a probably embellished "typical" menu, according to the *Ohio State Journal*, of roast beef, potatoes, stewed corn, beans, brown gravy, bread, coffee, and a dessert of dried peaches and apricot pie.[7] At night guards locked the wood barracks, but patrolled only three sides of the compound, the fourth being a cemetery the prisoners were loath to cross, according to one newspaper account.[8]

In Muskingum County, the approximately 175 prisoners from Mansfield Reformatory received almost equally refined attention. They slept in a large circus-style tent pitched on a hump of land that rose abruptly from level ground about two hundred yards from the Pike route at the intersection of the Sonora Road, six miles east of Zanesville. The first batch of Mansfield convicts had hardly passed through Zanesville on May

A truck typical of those used on the National Road project provides transportation for a convict work crew. *ODOT construction photos collection, Ohio History Connection Archives, Series 2203 AV*

31 when the Zanesville Ministerial Association met to organize a religious meeting at the prisoners' camp.[9] The following Sunday, and each Sunday thereafter through the summer, the ministers called together services at four p.m. at the camp, a diversion "greatly appreciated by the Mansfield men who listened with rapt attention and who seemed to be impressed and influenced by the messages," the Zanesville newspaper reported.[10] The first week of June the prisoners "warmly expressed their pleasure" when Mansfield Reformatory Chaplain H. W. Kellogg visited the camp.[11]

Sunday schedules also included another form of interaction with the community that the convicts actually sought: the reformatory prisoners had been in camp less than a month when they challenged local baseball teams to games. In the evenings and on weekends, the prisoners played organized baseball, including regularly scheduled Sunday morning battles between two segregated convict teams. Spectators from nearby farms witnessed one such contest that was reported by a local newspaper

Wheeling Avenue in Cambridge during 1918 construction. *Adair Collection, Cambridge, Ohio*

as "nip and tuck from the very start," including seventeen hits, three home runs, and only two errors, ending with the white team as 5–4 victors.[12]

But such communal spirit could not be sustained in the hard life of the work crews. On the night of July 8, paid workers Lubin Butler and James Boyd suffered gunshot wounds at the Snouffer Brothers Co. construction camp on the Pike. Butler, shot through the thigh, told police Boyd targeted him as Butler arose from his bunk. As Butler was being loaded onto the halted westbound Baltimore & Ohio (B&O) train to be taken for treatment, the wounded Boyd was seen attempting to board a train car and was taken into custody. Both men were aided at Bethesda Hospital in Zanesville.[13] Nor did cooler weather cool tempers: at the end of the summer, with baseball season completed and most players departed, Mansfield convict Joe Vuksic took a baseball bat to a fellow convict and "departed for parts unknown." He was not immediately apprehended.[14]

Clearly, life was by no means easy on the Pike. In August, record-breaking heat[15] baked convicts and paid laborers alike. Work documented by photography of the highway department and contemporary sources

Sledgehammers and Picks

Near Cambridge, a railroad worker drives a stake on the narrow-gauge B&O spur. Note that the rails stop about a hundred yards distant, and the roadway at this location has not yet been prepared. *David Adair Collection, Cambridge, Ohio*

refutes one local resident whose family remembers that "it was mostly hand work."[16] The pictures indeed show Black prisoners at work with hand tools, and every photograph from the National Road project that includes African Americans shows them bent over shovels, pulling rakes, or pushing wheelbarrows. White crew members, on the other hand, operated a surprising variety of mechanized industry. "Every modern and up-to-date piece of machinery fashioned for this kind of work is being used," reported the Zanesville *Times Recorder*.[17]

Use of machinery threatened worker safety, yet fortunately, and somewhat surprisingly, no deaths were reported during the National Road work in southeast Ohio. In late April, Contractor Burton had arranged for the services of Dr. Harry M. Rambo of Zanesville to treat illness or injury. Burton also alerted the local hospital and acquired the services of an ambulance for emergencies.[18] In mid-June medical care was

In a photo shot at the site of the previous image, bricks from the Burton & Townsend Brick Company are unloaded from a car on the railroad spur. Roadway preparation has not yet begun, although it appears curbs have been set in the distance, to the right. Bricks must have been delivered when they were ready, without waiting for the roadway to be prepared. *David Adair Collection, Cambridge, Ohio*

needed when a truck carrying foreman Albert Armbrister Sr., on its running boards squeezed Armbrister against a steam roller on the road project. The foreman, painfully injured with torn ligaments in his back and possible internal injuries, was taken to his Market Street home in Zanesville.[19] About a month later, a Mansfield convict working with a steam roller slipped and had his foot crushed beneath the roller. He was returned immediately to Mansfield.[20]

The machinery of the B&O railroad in Muskingum County greatly aided the project. One well-attested photo, for example, shows a classic scene captured somewhere west of New Concord at a narrow-gauge B&O rail spur that was assembled by B&O crews parallel to the road during early phases of measuring and grading. Modern local historians explain that rails snaked along the path of the Pike under construction from

Sledgehammers and Picks

Under summer sun, bricks are stacked and waiting, curbs have been poured, and some members of a construction work crew shovel gravel onto the prepared Pike roadway. *ODOT construction photos collection, Ohio History Connection Archives, Series 2203 AV*

Zanesville to as far as Cambridge in quarter-mile sections, with the receding sections lifted and carried forward.[21] A subsequent photo taken at the same location shows preparation for the road as first batches of bricks are delivered to an as-yet unimproved path. A surveyor can be seen to the right, while workers use hand tools in the foreground. The rails in the photos don't continue into the distance, but crews have set concrete curbs.

A railroad accompanying construction had assisted the earlier National Road rebuilding efforts from 1914 to 1916, so when the B&O railroad offered in April 1918 to lay down spurs and switches east of Zanesville, Contractor Burton surprised the highway department by saying in mid-May that the track "will not now be needed, in his judgment." A few days later, apparently after being chastised by the department, he reversed his position, writing to the B&O that "I...trust that we will get this switch in in time to be of much service to us...We are sorely in need of this track and I hope there will be no further delays." However, Burton's changed attitude did not mollify Chief Engineer Henry D.

Workers place bricks on the hard-packed surface of the National Road in Guernsey County. A marginal note includes the location and date 1917, which, if accurate, may indicate this image depicts workers with the Ayers & Kappes contract that preceded the Renick work in Guernsey County. *ODOT construction photos collection, Ohio History Connection Archives, Series 2203 AV*

Bruning. He complained that he had approved the rail siding as early as April 1, when he, Burton, and other field engineers visited the area. "There is not a consistent management in this improvement and more time should be given to the work by Mr. Burton himself," Bruning said.[22] Eventually crews completed two narrow-gauge sidings, one west of New Concord and another less usefully placed spur on the B. V. Moore farm about three-quarters of a mile north of the Pike route.[23]

Several photographs show thousands of bricks that had been offloaded from rail cars waiting while road foundations were laid down. Meanwhile crews would set up low wooden walls to create forms for the deep concrete curbs that defined the outside edges of the sixteen-foot-wide brick pavement. The forms were removed when the concrete curbs cured, and the prison crews filled the space between the curbs with coarse iron slag or rough limestone, broken up by hand and delivered in wheelbarrows. After steamrollers compacted about six inches of this cushion, prisoners put down layers of finer limestone or sand mixed with water. Steam rollers compacted this surface, and then craftsmen moved in to carefully lay the bricks in a durable pattern.

Laborers who were paid to work on the Pike became more expensive as the summer dragged on. Day laborers in Guernsey County in late June submitted a petition asking for a raise, and the Highway Advisory Board

Sledgehammers and Picks

A neighbor poses as concrete cures in forms along a rural section of the roadway. *ODOT construction photos collection, Ohio History Connection Archives, Series 2203 AV*

raised their pay from thirty-one cents to thirty-five cents per hour. In early July, Contractor Burton in Muskingum County returned to the board to ask once again for reimbursement to pay his son-in-law and a bookkeeping office staff, and the board once again put him off, demanding that he prepare a bill of those costs so they could review it later. Then in August, "wheel holders, drag scraper holders and dumpers, plow holders and snap drivers" in Guernsey County sought and received a twenty-five-cent per day increase in pay. This was necessary, Chief Engineer Bruning said, "to avoid disorganization,"[24] although he didn't define "organization" or the lack thereof. The convict crews got no such wage adjustments, even though the photographs show that managers, per standard operating procedures described by the Ohio Board of Administration, assigned most of the strenuous manual labor to the Black convicts who comprised the majority of the prison gangs.

Only a few guards supervised the convicts at the work sites, a situation that caused Highways Commissioner Cowen to worry about "leakage" of men and equipment.[25] In fact, records indicate that several convicts did

Some convict workers who walked away. Record of Escaped Prisoners, 1834–1935. *Ohio History Connection, State Archives Series 1363, BV7014; Ohio History Connection, Bertillon Cards with photographs, State Archives Series 1002 and 1416 AV*

William Tell, 33, a waiter from Pickaway County, Ohio, who had been incarcerated since 1905, left the work crew on the night of June 19.

Richard Style, 29, a sawmill worker in Lucas County, fled from Guernsey County work on July 3.

Albert Greene, 30, of Greene County, Ohio, walked away July 18, headed for home.

Harold Reynolds, 19, a Clark County, Ohio, burglar and Mansfield Reformatory inmate, walked away from the Muskingum County work site in June 1918.

Mansfield Reformatory inmate J. P. Justice, 20, of Sedalia, Mississippi, charged with carrying a concealed weapon in Lorain, Ohio, walked away from the Muskingum County work in June 1918.

John Snyder, 27, a Canton hat maker, walked away from the Muskingum County work in June 1918. He had been sentenced to Mansfield Reformatory for forging an $11.50 check.

Sledgehammers and Picks

A convict crew works at a limestone quarry in Guernsey County. In the background, two guards watch. Note shovels and sledgehammers strewn about. *ODOT construction photos collection, Ohio History Connection Archives, Series 2203 AV*

bolt from the National Road project, despite Governor Cox's recollection that only one prisoner misbehaved.[26] For example, the Mansfield Reformatory inmates proved to be especially inclined to walk away from the projects: new Mansfield prison laborers had hardly settled into their circus-tent bunks when Arthur Brown, Clinton Swords, Tony Berek, and Matt Koko walked away on or before June 5.[27] J. P. Justice, John Snyder, and Harold Reynolds left the Muskingum County work site a few days later, and on June 12 a German immigrant prisoner named Kirschner escaped. The Columbus *Evening Dispatch* reported that William Tell, alias Alford Knox, left the Guernsey County work area the night of June 19 and was not immediately returned. Prison records indicate that George Miller, 30, convicted of shooting to wound in Marion County, Ohio, and Richard Style, both from Lucas County, Ohio, fled on July 3. (Unlike most walkaways, who were quickly returned, Miller was not apprehended until 1931, and served prison time until 1965.) John Scales of Mahoning County, Ohio, walked away on July 5; Albert Greene, 43, left for his home near Xenia, Ohio, without leave July 18 but was returned by Dayton authorities

Gravel is distributed by shovel in one of the final paving steps. In the background, tar is being heated. *ODOT construction photos collection, Ohio History Connection Archives, Series 2203 AV*

a week later; and Mike Yakovich, a member of the crews who had been convicted of carrying a concealed weapon in Summit County, Ohio, walked away July 31. Baseball batter Joe Vuksic fled on October 11. In one odd twist, a fugitive joined the project: police arrested draft dodger Cassadia Mazzola at a camp where he was masquerading as a worker.[28]

The great majority of prisoners from the Ohio Penitentiary and Mansfield Reformatory stayed on the job, and in terms of the actual quality of the convict labor, pure numbers show the state got its money's worth. In the highway engineer's monthly report to the Highway Advisory Board, dated June 18, 1918, resident engineer Dwight L. Moorehead reported that more than two hundred Ohio Penitentiary convicts had arrived in Guernsey County by mid-May, and by early June they had unloaded 12,500 bricks, quarried 2,600 cubic yards of sandstone, unloaded five train carloads of sand and twelve carloads of slag (part of five thousand tons of this was steel production byproduct purchased for road base cushion at six cents per ton from the Carnegie Steel Company of Pittsburgh). Ten thousand feet of concrete berms had been partly completed, Moorehead added.

Sledgehammers and Picks

Workers pause while pouring tar binder on the road prior to the final layer of fine sand and bricking. *ODOT construction photos collection, Ohio History Connection Archives, Series 2203 AV*

In another section, crews toiled on the property of L. P. Moore, who had arranged with Harness Renick to sell limestone to the state. First, laborers had to remove twenty-four thousand cubic yards of overburden dirt and rock—enough to fill more than seven Olympic-sized swimming pools—to uncover a five-foot-thick limestone ledge as long as a football field and half as wide.[29] The photo on page 65 shows just such a prison crew at work in Guernsey County, possibly in this limestone quarry. Sledgehammers and picks wielded by convicts pulverized the stone, which was hauled away on horse-drawn rail carts and eventually deposited as the bottom cushion on the roadbed.

According to prison records and contemporary accounts, many of the Black prisoners had migrated to Ohio from the Deep South, which would have made them early members of the Great Migration of Black Americans seeking work in the North during The Great War and for some years afterward.[30] (One of these men was J. P. Justice, of Sedalia, Missis-

A final layer of sand distributed. *ODOT construction photos collection, Ohio History Connection Archives, Series 2203 AV*

sippi, one of the Mansfield inmates who fled the Muskingum County camp in June.) As such, many of them had been raised in a culture of gospel music and call-and-response work chants, a melodious tradition these laborers likely shared as they made the quarry echo with the ringing of sledgehammers crushing stone.

Progress slowed after raw materials arrived at road-building sites. In August, advisory board member Dudley S. Humphrey reported to the board that he had "motored over National Road from Columbus to Zanesville," where he met Contractor Burton. The contractor and brick executive had just hosted a tour of the work with the monthly meeting of the Ohio Paving Brick Association, and that group, including "prominent representatives of the paving industry,"[31] must have emboldened Burton, because the contractor spewed complaints to Humphrey about lack of progress. County Engineer Ralph Strait "is not playing quite fair," Burton said, and supplies weren't arriving from the highway department. Humphrey determined to see for himself.

Sledgehammers and Picks

"After quite careful inspection over the whole road," Humphrey told the board, "I am quite concerned as to getting the work done in reasonable season this fall." He explained that supervisors attended to the work sites sporadically, allowing useless grading, improperly placed supplies, and widespread inefficiencies. "Renick is very much behind, and will have to prove up better to get through this fall," Humphrey said.

"Altogether too much hand-work is being done," Humphrey observed. "Better equipment in the way of tools would get the work done much faster and save money."[32]

Dynamite was a quick and necessary tool to move forward on the Pike. Contractor Burton ordered $368 worth of dynamite on June 3 and another $178 shipment in early July, without the highway department's prior approval, but the board paid the bills after its members voiced complaints, and then the state ordered another one thousand pounds of dynamite and forty kegs of blasting powder at $2.35 per keg. It must have given highway department leaders pause to have to acquire such munitions, when at the time more than three hundred convicts were working along about twenty-five miles of roadway. Nevertheless, in September the state approved purchase of another thirty-four cases of dynamite and thirty-two kegs of blasting powder, along with assorted blasting caps, fuses, and associated materials.

The effects were dramatic to at least one observer. "How the red clay flew in those hills of southeastern Ohio!" Governor Cox recalled in his memoirs. "The countryside shook from the explosions of dynamite that were tearing away rock and hardpan soil."[33]

VII

Victory Declared

OHIO PENITENTIARY WARDEN Preston Thomas had grandiose ideas by the end of the summer of 1918. The more than three hundred Black convict laborers from his institution had performed so well on the National Road project that he announced expansive plans to become the state's general contractor for highway construction the following year. Apparently forgetting that he had on March 19 boasted of driving on a completed National Road by the Fourth of July, six months later he critiqued the leadership of the road project as a problem he alone could fix.

"All that I will ask will be that I be furnished with the necessary specifications and be told the amount of road that is desired to be constructed, and I will go ahead and build it with prison labor," he said during Labor Day weekend. "The trouble with the present system of using prisoners in road building in the state is that they are under outside supervision.... By supervising the building of the roads myself I could take a couple of hundred prisoners, build a camp and have them under direct supervision all the time."[1] In reality, since the roads were public services, the warden's vision would have constituted a state account system, forbidden by Ohio's Wertz law.

As highway board member Humphrey had reported, Warden Thomas's attitude toward the National Road's project supervisors wasn't too far from accurate. In mid-August, Contractor Burton sought assurances from the board that he would be paid if work continued and costs

Victory Declared

exceeded the money originally appropriated for the Muskingum County work. Chief Engineer Bruning calculated that yes, another $35,000 would be needed, so the board set aside $35,000–just short of $600,000 in today's money—to assure Burton. Three weeks later the board approved a proposal that paid a contractor a fee of 25 percent for work completed by November 1, and 15 percent for work completed after that date, thus formally recognizing it wasn't going to get its finished highway by the end of summer. The board stipulated, however, that "a competent superintendent" would have to be on the job, paid $200 per month.

Highway Department Commissioner Cowen and his advisory board must have been scanning their maps uncomfortably as they felt the eyes of Governor Cox peering over their shoulders. He had delivered a Labor Day speech in Cambridge—surely an unacknowledged inspection visit—during which he emphasized Ohio's leadership in providing workmen's compensation and thanked workers for their cooperation during the war.[2] The governor only had to look east or west to see stacked bricks, construction equipment, a badly rutted detour running from Zanesville south through the hamlets of Chandlersville and Rix Mills, and dust in the air around the unfinished National Road. The highway department was losing its laborers, too. In mid-August the Mansfield Reformatory granted parole to thirty of the convicts working in Muskingum County. They sent papers to them in the field and didn't even require them to return to the reformatory for processing.[3] Then in mid-September the Ohio Penitentiary parole board released about fifty of the prisoners who had been working on the Road, amid great praise for them. "The work of the men has been done in a most satisfactory manner," reported the Columbus *Sunday Dispatch*.[4]

The locals were getting impatient, as well. Military "truck trains" of thirty to forty vehicles were beginning to pass through Zanesville and continue on the half-built pike and the Chandlersville-Rix Mills detour.[5] Seeing the sixteen-mile expanse of brick between Zanesville and New Concord nearing completion, the business leaders of the city made a long-distance telephone call to Columbus at the end of September. The time had come, they said, to close the detour and open up commerce again. The state relented: "The improvement of the National Road between Zanesville and New Concord will be completed this week, and

A resident poses on the section of the National Road called Dewey Avenue, southwest of downtown Cambridge, after some concrete curbs have been set. *Adair Collection, Cambridge, Ohio*

dedicatory exercises will be held by the Zanesville board of trade next week," announced Highway Advisory Board president McCulloch on Monday, September 30.

As was typical in National Road project predictions, however, his time frame was optimistic. A week later, the Zanesville Board of Trade and Contractor Burton were still planning proper dedication ceremonies, even while a serious auto accident on the completed portion of the Pike near Zanesville injured two Columbus residents and punctuated public anticipation of the new highway.[6] Motorists finally rolled onto the new pavement on Monday, October 14, and the town fathers scheduled elaborate formal opening ceremonies. A Liberty Loan Bond Sale delayed the speechifying for a week, but officials set the date for late October.

This announcement of the ribbon-cutting amounted to highway officials throwing up their hands and declaring victory with a large, unstated addendum. The distance from Zanesville to New Concord amounted to about two-thirds of the National Road mileage that had to be rebuilt from

Young observers watch as the National Road, known as Wheeling Avenue in downtown Cambridge, gets its layer of bricks. *Adair Collection, Cambridge, Ohio*

scratch, and it was all in Muskingum County. In Guernsey County, bricking continued on the National Road route through the county seat, Cambridge, and the community of Old Washington had requested and partially funded renovation of the Pike within its town limits. Progress elsewhere on the Pike in Guernsey County evaporated.

The National Council of Defense once again stepped in, requesting that Cambridge quickly finish bricking the portion of the National Road within its town limits.[7]

The lack of progress further east, near Old Washington, so alarmed the State Highway Board that its president, H. R. McCulloch, visited the job site in person. With the grand opening ceremonies just days away, he returned to report to Highway Commissioner Cowen that "practically no progress [was] being made." A dozen horse teams at the limestone quarry east of Old Washington stood idle, lack of repairs had rendered the steam shovel on the Road inoperable, and the work was being mismanaged by an "incompetent" supervisor while contractor Harness Renick "had discontinued giving the job his personal attention." McCulloch's report so incensed Cowen that he once again called Renick in for a personal dressing-down at the Highway Advisory Board meeting. Two days before the grand opening ceremonies, members of the board expressed their dissatisfaction and told Renick in unmistakable terms that the National Road project required his personal attention; he responded by assuring them that he would fire the incompetent superintendent and handle the job personally. The project would be completed "as rapidly as possible," he said.[8]

VIII

The Last Brick

There was a rough and rocky road beds
along the National Pike
It was here that trucks have broken down
and men have had to hike.
As soldier boys go thru now no mud holes wreck their day
So it's here in dear New Concord that we dedicate this way.

THE MUSKINGUM COLLEGE Glee Club sang this ditty, written to celebrate the completion of the rebuilt National Road in southeast Ohio, on October 23, 1918, at the S bridge just west of New Concord. Some five thousand citizens of southeast Ohio had gathered at ceremonies organized by Contractor Rufus Burton, including anyone who had anything to do with the project, from Governor Cox and his wife, to state auditor Victor Donahey, to district congressman George White and all the members of the Ohio Highway Department Advisory Board. Muskingum College President Knox Montgomery attended, as did a representative of the Good Roads Federation and an officer of the Ohio Paving Block Manufacturers Association. Bands played, there was a community sing-along, and dozens of motor cars from as far away as Columbus lined up to try out the new pavement. The perfect autumn weather, brisk and clear but a bit cloudy later in the day, capped the day's activities.[1]

Burton initiated the National Road project closing ceremonies at the same place where the undertaking had begun, beneath the ornate ceiling of the Clarendon Hotel's dining room in Zanesville. The contractor who

An Ohio Highways Department photo dated 1918, probably recording the October 23 ceremonies on the S bridge just west of New Concord, Ohio. An estimated five thousand people, including Ohio Governor James M. Cox, celebrated completion of the rebuilt National Road. Participants were asked to drive to the event on a chill day with their car tops down, and as the photo shows some did, but many did not. *Ohio Department of Transportation construction photos collection, Ohio History Connection Archives, Series 2203 AV*

had wrestled with the highway department throughout the summer hosted about seventy-five dignitaries at a luncheon there, followed by music from a local band. The community invitation had gone out to "every owner of a machine" to join an auto parade directed by marshal and Zanesville retailer W. E. Deacon, who positioned the motor cars of visiting officials first, followed by machines of the National League of Women's Service, representatives of the Alpha Motoring Club, the cars of the Muskingum Motor Club and visiting autos.[2] Then, at the close of the luncheon, "hundreds of the residents of Zanesville," as well as the visitors from Columbus, cranked their motor cars to life and drove—tops down and tonneau covers removed, by request—about fourteen miles in a winding procession over the new brick pavement to the west side of New Concord, where they were met by thousands of residents in the midst of "celebration and jollification."[3]

The Last Brick 77

Burton served as master of ceremonies for an afternoon during which all significant players got their chance to speak. Three common threads wove through the messages: the lengthy history and importance to commerce of the Cumberland Pike; its importance as an artery of national security and the war effort; and appreciation of the work of the convict laborers who helped accomplish the task in record time. Conveniently ignored were the half-dozen miles of road around Old Washington yet to be paved.

As befitted his status as a scholar, Muskingum College President Montgomery lectured the audience on the history of the National Road. H. R. McCulloch, chair of the highway department advisory board and a resident of Cambridge, continued with a reference to Ebenezer Zane and the other historic National Road builders who had laid its foundation both literally and metaphorically. McCulloch added frank comments about challenges and disappointments the board had encountered through the summer, but he noted that sixteen miles of road through Muskingum County had been completed in five months, which he called a record in road construction. And the accomplishment could not have happened, he said, without convict labor. "Without their aid the work could not have been done in such a short time," he said. "But they did it willingly and patriotically."[4]

With Americans fighting in Europe even as they spoke, the politicians who followed at the podium shared muted comments. Congressman White marveled at the speed of construction and remarked about the federal-state cooperation that had enabled the project. He recalled how roads had relieved rail congestion earlier in the year and hailed the advantages of good roads to the farmer and the consumer. The improved National Road would be good for parcel post truck service now, he added.

The highlight of the day had to be eight-year-old Harriet Burton Dodd, granddaughter of Rufus Burton, who at the appointed moment handed a ceremonial paving brick to Governor James Cox. First, however, Burton provided his own assessment of Cox, earned after a summer of disputes with the governor, a fellow Democrat: "He has proven himself more of a businessman than a politician, and has had much to do with the improvement of the National Road."[5]

Cox answered that he appreciated the opportunity to attend the opening ceremonies and confirmed the importance of the revived road for commerce in Muskingum and Guernsey Counties. The state had responded to the request of the government, he said, even though the difficult project presented many challenges. He added that the work would not have been possible without the help of the "boys" from Mansfield Reformatory who had been put to work in Muskingum County, despite criticism that their employment violated the law.

"The law, it is true, did not specifically provide for the employment of these men on the work," he said, "but it did not prohibit it, simply because such an emergency was never before faced."[6]

Cox said he called upon the inmates from the Ohio Penitentiary and Mansfield Reformatory after the federal government issued "an S.O.S. call," and he saluted the loyalty of the convicts, who had "reclaimed themselves" and in many cases had been rewarded with paroles. He emphasized that the project they had completed would help the war effort and support the troops heading overseas.

Cox concluded his remarks with praise for the officials of Muskingum and Guernsey Counties, the contractors who had supervised the work, and Burton. Then he and the members of the advisory board laid the final brick in place on the S bridge, and President Montgomery stepped in to invite motorists in the crowd to tour the Muskingum College campus across town. Many accepted his offer, while others fired up their vehicles and drove about nine miles east on the Pike to Cambridge, the terminus of the bricked pavement at that point.

The motor car traffic that day, with dozens of puttering, smoky, open-topped cars full of finely dressed citizens, must have been a curious sight for the dusty crews doing the remaining cleanup work along the roadway. They would continue waving at sight-seeing motorists for the rest of the week and through the weekend, when good weather and removal of a ban on Sunday driving brought out "hundreds of machines," traveling from as far away as Columbus. In New Concord, 205 automobiles passed during one fifteen-minute span, according to the *Daily Jeffersonian* newspaper.[7] Unfortunately, the pavement also attracted a livelier crowd. Within days the local newspaper published a complaint in an anti-liquor editorial: "On last Saturday the road was altogether unsafe for legitimate traffic, and at no time can one be assured that some intoxicated driver or bunch of 'joy' riders will not play havoc with his rightful pursuits."[8]

The Last Brick 79

More legitimate traffic champed at the mechanical bit as well. The weekend after the opening ceremony a mail truck made a test run between Zanesville and Cambridge, and shortly thereafter Ira P. Dawson, the agent for the postmaster general's motor truck delivery, met with the Cambridge postmaster to plan upcoming motor deliveries. They decided regular postal truck routes on the Road would start November 10, with service to Wheeling to begin when Renick's work crews completed the National Road through Old Washington in Guernsey County.[9]

On November 8, a caravan of thirty-three army trucks—the reason the Pike had been rebuilt—stopped in Cambridge after riding the Pike from Springfield through Zanesville the day before. The men of the Army Corps Ambulance Sanitary Train No. 239 slept in the McMahon building on Seventh Street in Cambridge and had breakfast the following day in the basement of the First Methodist Episcopal Church before continuing east.[10]

It is highly doubtful the Army Corps ambulances made it to the East Coast before news arrived: in France, at the eleventh hour of the eleventh day of November 1918, an armistice was signed to end The Great War. Likely somewhere along the National Road in Pennsylvania or Maryland the caravan's drivers and crews heard the news and stopped to celebrate.

IX

Settling Accounts

EVEN THOUGH THE supposed last brick had been dropped into the pavement of the National Road just west of New Concord, the members of the Ohio Highway Department Advisory Board returned to Columbus to face continuing difficulties with the National Road project. Several miles of road around Old Washington in Guernsey County awaited completion, and although the immediate need for war matériel had dissipated, the interstate value of the Pike would be greatly lessened if traffic bogged down in eastern Ohio. In addition, as a war measure the federal government had ordered a halt to deliveries of road-building supplies, and the highway department had to get assurances that current work crews and supplies would be sufficient to continue.

Then the weather turned sour. Temperatures dropped to near freezing most days, and below freezing many nights, a misery for the remaining Ohio Penitentiary convicts in their unheated bunk house and the Mansfield Reformatory inmates in their tent. During the second week of December more than an inch of rain fell over two days.[1] Work had to be suspended, and Board President McCulloch warned that regardless of the weather the prison laborers had to be busy, and if they were not working, they would have to be returned to their institutions.

The contractors still directing work crews near Old Washington had to continue without prisoner labor because the Ohio Prison Board of Administration was loath to pay convicts who weren't working. Most of

Settling Accounts

them had been recalled, anyway: the state had upheld the governor's promise to reward positive industry of prison laborers and issued parole or outright freedom to many. As early as the first week of August some thirty Mansfield Reformatory inmates had been released, and a month later about fifty state penitentiary prisoners working in Guernsey County were granted parole. Prison records show that on October 28, William Jones, 32, of Cuyahoga County in northern Ohio, was granted conditional release, and Arthur Sanders, 35, of Cuyahoga County, was granted parole. Charles Irving, 38, of Pickaway County got conditional release two days later; Will "Deacon" Curry, 46, of Lawrence County and Leroy Lucas, 28, of Belmont County, were paroled November 20. On November 22, a busy parole board released Luke Stewart, convicted of carrying a concealed weapon, and convicted burglars Charles Davis, Albert Baily and Charles Rice, all of whom had been imprisoned the same day in September, 1917. John Johnson, 33, of Jefferson County, William Watkins, 35, of Lucas County, Clyde Wyatt, 27, and John Gheeter, 39, of Cuyahoga County, Ed McGraw, 35, of Lucas County, Frank Henderson, 34, of Mahoning County, Warren Newman, 30, and Jacob Wheeler, 48, both of Hamilton County, were paroled on November 25. In December parole was given to Curtis Mason, 26, of Hamilton County, John Johnson, 31, of Cuyahoga County, William Walton and James Pleasant, 24, while John Washington, Charles Archer and Ed Taylor, all of Cuyahoga County, were granted conditional release, according to existing records. In total, more than a third of the total number of Black inmates from the Ohio State Penitentiary who were enlisted to work on the National Road received outright pardons, conditional release, or parole.

Sadly, many of the Mansfield Reformatory prisoners left dirt and sweat in Muskingum County only to encounter deadly conditions in the institution. Superintendent Thomas Jenkins had warned the board of administration in early October that prisoners were about to return from their National Road work camp even while "the epidemic of Spanish flu has reached Mansfield, the report being that there are five hundred cases developed in the last three days." Inside the institution, the situation worsened: inmate John Dennis died October 18, and nineteen-year-old Morgan Kerwick died four days later. By the end of October, fourteen prisoners had died, and dozens more were bedridden. Jenkins himself fell ill for three days in mid-October.[2] On the last day of the month he was able to report from his office, having improved considerably, but the news from his institution was not good: "I regret exceedingly that conditions have become so serious in our institution, but am at a loss to know what we can do," he wrote. "...boys persist in throwing back the covers when they get too warm and of getting out on the sides of their cots. Slight as this exposure is, it seems to be sufficient to add to their troubles and death seems to be the only relief." But the prison doctor added that conditions were improving, and by mid-November fatalities stopped, with a total of twenty inmates lost to the Spanish flu.

Back in Guernsey County, conditions were less physically dire, but financially troubled. With work proceeding at a snail's pace, representatives for contractors Ferguson & Edmondson visited the Highway Advisory Board's December 17 meeting to request that the board clarify their status. The board agreed to keep them under contract and then turned to the matter of their payment, because the highway department's coffers had run dry. The board decided to move $14,000 in maintenance funds— more than $700,000 in today's money—"to meet payrolls and liabilities," noted Commissioner Cowen. "There is at present no other available fund," he added.

The state had to do some dickering to settle up in Muskingum County. O. N. Townsend, who headed Burton & Townsend Brick Company with Contractor Burton, visited the board with James R. Marker, president of the Ohio Brick Manufacturers' Association, to complain about the way the state had computed the number of bricks actually used versus the leftovers and broken pieces, called *culls*. Townsend said his company had supplied 5,007,250 bricks, and their estimated count yielded 95,000 culls. The state, on the other hand, had sent people to make an actual count of bricks used at a dozen places in Muskingum County, and determined that fewer bricks had been needed. The brickmakers complained that by custom they counted forty bricks per square yard; the Highway board split the difference, offering to pay for 47,500 leftover and broken bricks.

The miles of new brick pavement in southeast Ohio became an integral part of a significant transportation artery. Recognition by the private National Old Trails Association, motorists' guides (a mapping innovation

Settling Accounts

A section of the brick-paved National Road today, preserved in Muskingum County as Brick Road. The pavement is sixteen feet wide, between concrete curbs.
Photo by Jeffrey Alan John

begun in part by B. F. Goodrich's Raymond Beck), and new paving all the way from Cumberland, Maryland, to Indianapolis beckoned postwar motorists. One important publication, *The Official Automobile Blue Book*, described the National Pike as "greatly improved and easily followed."[3]

In 1911, Rep. Douglas, his wife, and driver challenged the coarse, uneven National Road on their five-day adventure from Washington to Chillicothe, Ohio, in his Ford Model T. Nine years later, in June, 1920, five ladies embarked on a similar trip on the National Road, traveling in a two-year-old Dodge from Corydon, Indiana, eastward to Washington, DC. As detailed by the driver, Mrs. Henry Wiseman, in a 1920 *Hoosier Motorist* article,[4] the group found the newly paved route through eastern Ohio's hills "perfectly smooth." Ultimately the ladies toured the east from Virginia north to Niagara Falls—2,500 miles in seventeen days—marred only on the first, third, and fifteenth days by flat tires that they fixed themselves. "Second tire change we changed in 10 minutes—the last one in seven minutes. Everyone had a certain part in tire changing and knew their job," Mrs. Wiseman proudly reported.[5]

Such were the hazards of motor travel on the National Road in the 1920s. The well-prepared motorist was expected to carry extra tires, inner tubes and patches, spark plugs, and even a shovel and rope.[6] Entrepreneurs soon recognized the market for servicing afflicted members of the traveling public who weren't as handy as the Indiana women, and by 1930 gas stations had sprouted everywhere along the National Road to fix tires or make repairs. And where once-adventurous motorists could park along the roadway to picnic or even pitch a tent overnight, now motor courts and diners interrupted the countryside. One camp near Zanesville, Ohio, charged "50 cents for tables under roof, and shower." Farther east, Star Camp charged fifty cents, with shower and bath ten cents extra.[7]

By 1921, the federal government had officially recognized the importance of the automobile in American life. State highway construction budgets rose to $633 million by 1920, and 8.1 million automobiles and trucks were registered that year.[8] In Indiana, one out of every six persons owned a car.[9] Although Logan Page, the Progressive head of the Bureau of Public Roads, died unexpectedly in 1918 (and with him Progressive zeal for scientifically constructed good roads), the Federal Highway Act of 1921 created a system of funding to encourage "an adequate and connected system of highways, interstate in character."[10] Two years later, the federal government adopted a national numbering system under which east–west routes were designated with even numbers, while north–south routes received odd numbers. Road crews fanned out to install now-familiar white, shield-shaped signs on the road variously known as Ohio 1, The National Old Trails Road, the National Road, the National Pike, or the Cumberland Road. Officially renamed US Route 40, it became part of a system of 164,000 miles, carrying almost twenty million cars and trucks in 1925.[11]

Motoring remained a national passion even through the Great Depression of the 1930s. With continuous funding available, Route 40 was repaved with asphalt in 1932, "on the theory that it would not only provide better resiliency, but would also provide a darker road to protect motorists' eyes,"[12] In addition, the route was not only widened from its

Settling Accounts

Fox Creek S Bridge today. The newer route of the National Road passes to the left, adjacent to the old route. *Photo by Jeffrey Alan John*

narrow sixteen-foot pavement to three or four lanes, but also straightened to eliminate its former meandering path, which originally followed a trail used by wildlife and the people who pursued them. Now US Route 40 motorists cruising at thirty miles per hour found a smooth, straight, and relatively level way and the convenience of rest areas with real running water, unlike the former experience of drinking from roadside springs.

The new, fast highway featured motor lodges, tourist camps, and taverns such as the Neil House in downtown Columbus, Ohio, across from the Statehouse; the Pennsylvania House near Springfield, Ohio; or the Century Inn in Scenery Hill, Pennsylvania, that filled at night and emptied in the morning. Fruit stands, antique shops, and hamburger joints dotted roadsides. "The Road is a virtual shopper's lane," exclaimed author and Route 40 traveler Philip Jordan in 1947. He related the complaint of one Maryland old-timer along the old road: "'Stop anywhere along the pike an' you'll be in front of a signboard or a guy tryin' to sell you somthin. It didn't used ter be thataway.'"[13]

World War II brought gasoline rationing and a temporary slowdown on Route 40. Military vehicles and commercial trucking continued to use the Pike, but few civilians had sufficient "A" ration stickers to take extended tours. Life was renewed after 1945, however, as gasoline flowed, tourists returned, and Route 40 became a major artery across the country again.

"The old road has become a hurried, neurotic highway," complained Jordan.

That is, until it was replaced by Interstate 70. The National Road, "Main Street of America," reached the height of its use in 1960, just as construction of the interstate began in Ohio. The new route extended to Columbus by 1968, and the following year it was opened eastward to Zanesville. Interstate planners frequently laid the new highway parallel to the National Road, and sometimes on top of it outright, burying miles of old asphalt and brick pavement. Meanwhile the remaining roadway of Route 40, bypassed and obsolete, returned to secondary status.

X

Winners and Losers

ULTIMATELY, WHO BENEFITED from the National Road construction project of 1918? Who lost? Fundamentally, the vastly improved road advanced commerce in Muskingum and Guernsey Counties, bringing modern transportation to the foothills of the Appalachians. Truck transport and mail delivery came immediately, not to mention automobile touring by ordinary citizens.

In the elections of November 1918, the citizenry narrowly chose Governor James M. Cox as the only Democrat to win a statewide seat in Ohio. The GOP won the offices of Lieutenant Governor and Secretary of State and took control of the Ohio legislature. World War I ended within days after the votes were counted, and the new Republican-led legislature took that as its cue to turn gimlet eyes toward the governor's Progressive agenda. Funds for road building, including the National Road project, became a target of scrutiny.

By December of that year motor cars were helping to settle in the new brick pavement along miles of National Road in Muskingum and Guernsey Counties, with one small exception. East of Old Washington about a mile of roadway remained as only compacted sand, lacking bricks until well into the winter. This stretch of construction was under the supervision of contractor Harness Renick. The new legislature took notice.

Renick had been awarded a National Road contract in eastern Guernsey County under a force account in October 1917. Prior to that time, as early as 1914, the Office of Public Roads began to cooperate with the states in order to create better roads, and the Zanesville firm of Ayres & Kappes initially won the 1914 contract. According to the findings of a joint investigative committee of the legislature in 1919, Ayers & Kappes won the job with a bid of $331,000 for thirteen miles of bricked roadway, and although its work had been slowed by the familiar lack of supplies and labor due to the war, their crews had completed more than 92 percent of the work and had been paid all but $30,000 of the contract by October 1917.

Then, according to the investigation, the state highway commissioner abruptly ended the Ayers & Kappes contract and awarded a force account contract for the remainder of the work to Renick, allowing 10 percent commission above costs, rental fees for Renick's equipment at fifty cents per hour, as well as drivers' wages for about twenty teams of Renick horses. (Five months later, similar force accounts would be enacted for Burton's work in Muskingum County.) About 1.5 miles of roadway remained to be completed.

The investigations committee withheld no punches in its report to the legislature: "Your committee finds that the 'force account' contractor expended money recklessly and without regard for the simplest of business methods," the committee reported, "and that he consumed 1 year and 28 days in constructing 1 1/2 miles of roadway, and that he was paid by the state highway department $78,753.05. Adding to this amount the cost of engineering supervision charged against the job, it cost the state of Ohio $80,550.57 to construct one and a half miles of the simplest type of brick pavement.

"Your committee does not deem it necessary to go into detail and set forth each and every act of mismanagement," the legislators fumed. They concluded that the highway commissioner had fired the original contractors Ayers & Kappes without justification, and the highway department had allowed costs to "accumulate beyond reason" through "gross negligence and inefficient expenditure of funds."[1]

If the cost of Renick's work offended the Republican-led legislature that much, total costs to the state for the entire National Road rebuilding project in both Muskingum and Guernsey Counties truly caused conniptions. The Zanesville *Times Recorder* complained that the "cost plus percentages" method of calculating payment in Muskingum County

Winners and Losers

upped the final cost from Contractor Rufus Burton's originally approved $469,000 to about $700,000. Governor Cox had brought the entire project to the county commissioners as a war emergency, costs be damned, but according to local historian Norris Schneider, the governor at a meeting convened days after the closing ceremonies was told to his dismay that the federal government had not declared the project as an authentic emergency. Washington wouldn't budge beyond its originally agreed-upon $10,000 per mile input.[2] Between March 1 and December 31, 1918, invoices, bills, and various charges approved by the highway department advisory committee, very roughly calculated, came to a total of about $1,367,000, or more than $23 million in today's money. The counties sold bonds to fund their share ($294,000 in Muskingum County alone, in 1918 dollars) but even counting the extremely low-cost convict labor, at a total of more than $115,300 (about $2 million in 2020 dollars) per mile, the twenty-four-mile National Road rebuilding project in Muskingum and Guernsey Counties had not been much of a bargain, and the state was on the hook for more than $2 million in 1918 dollars.

The state legislature, no doubt alarmed by the huge sums spent in the National Road project, targeted the Department of Highways. As one of the state's administrative agencies run by Cox-appointed officials, it was reorganized by the legislature in its "Act to establish an administrative code for the State, to create new administrative departments and redistribute among them existing administrative functions," enacted in July of 1921. It abolished the office of Commissioner of Highways, eliminated the Highways Advisory Board, and subsumed the highway department under a director of public works who was responsible for state highways, state-owned buildings and grounds, canals, and the leasing of state offices. "It may be a debatable question whether the single director, changeable with each change of governor, is the proper form of headship for the department of public works, in view of the need for preserving continuity of policy in highway administration," one contemporary observer noted.[3] (Six years later the legislature reverted to the previous form, remaking the hybrid administration into separate departments of highways and public works.)

The state never pursued Harness Renick for his inefficiencies. He continued as a road construction contractor, with jobs in Ohio and Pennsylvania, until his death at age seventy-three in 1944 in Circleville, Ohio.

Runaway expenses proved unpopular with state legislators, to say the least. Highway Commissioner Clinton Cowen left his post in 1919 under a cloud of legislative criticism, and the highway department advisory board members had their chairs pulled out from under them when the board was abolished in 1921.

In Muskingum County, Contractor Rufus C. Burton had pledged to work without compensation, but his firm Burton & Townsend sold more than five million bricks to the state and charged for them down to the last culls. His son-in-law served as his bookkeeper, at $150 per month.

After he organized the last-brick celebration and served as its master of ceremonies, Burton continued as a distinguished member of the Zanesville community. He served on the boards of directors for several local banks and a coal company, and after he retired from the Burton-Townsend Brick Company Burton dabbled in real estate. "As a loyal booster of Zanesville he had no peer," noted his obituary in 1928 on the front page of the *Times Recorder*.[4] He was seventy-two when he died, surrounded by his family in his mansion in Zanesville.

The road construction operation run by Burton, Renick, and their sub-contractors benefited dozens of individuals as well. Some of Harness Renick' landowner friends in Guernsey County benefited—including L. P. Moore, S. M. Smith, and Ella F. George, with whom Renick dealt for sand, limestone, and access rights. In addition, the project brought hundreds of jobs—more than could be filled in wartime—for laborers, team drivers, and craftspeople such as brick layers and concrete finishers, who earned regular state paychecks.

For more than three hundred prison inmates, whether they actually "volunteered" or were pressed into service, National Road labor provided a hard diversion outside the walls of institutions. Contemporary photographs show convict laborers assigned to backbreaking tasks. They shared crude living quarters and earned miserable pennies per day wages. Nevertheless, the prisoners earned honest accolades for record-breaking accomplishments, with relatively few choosing to run away from their work crews. By the end of the project, about a third of the convict workers had received paroles or early release.

Preston E. Thomas, Ohio State Penitentiary Warden, held that position far longer than any other warden at the "Big House." Having been

Winners and Losers

appointed by Cox in 1913, he continued in his post for twenty-two years. The long tenure of Warden Thomas pivoted dramatically on Easter Monday of 1930. About 5:30 that afternoon, convicts playing cards saw smoke and fire in the upper reaches of the penitentiary's cell blocks G and H, but guards dithered as they tried to determine whether this was one of the relatively common nuisance fires ignited by inmates in their bedding to smoke out bedbugs, or something more. Within minutes fumes filled the prison, although on the porch of his comfortable quarters Warden Thomas didn't smell anything because of an asthma condition, he claimed later. "I lost my smeller several years ago," Thomas told a board of inquiry. "I can't smell a skunk. I'm not kidding."[5] The warden later testified that he sought assurances that the Columbus Fire Department had been called, and then, being loath to enter the prison yard without bodyguards, he went outside the walls to guard against escapees. Inside the prison, guards debated whether to open prisoners' cells while the fire spread. Within hours, 322 prisoners died.

For more than a week after the conflagration, about 1,300 convicts roamed freely among the smoldering ruins inside the prison walls. They refused guards' demands to return to undamaged cells, and made their attitude toward Thomas clear: "Send the warden out here and we'll tear him to pieces," one of them told officials who had ventured into the wreck;[6] in an interview with *Columbus Evening Dispatch* reporters, inmate Charles Quinlan of Cuyahoga County warned of "a path of passive resistance that will be rigidly adhered to so long as P. E. Thomas remains warden of the Ohio penitentiary.... Do not let the warden show his face in here."[7] To mollify the surviving prison population, the Ohio attorney general recommended a temporary suspension of Warden Thomas, to which Thomas replied that communist sympathizers were ringleaders. "This is a giving away of the part of regularly constituted government to the demands of the 'red-shirt' element," he said.

Ultimately Ohio Governor Myers Cooper took no action to remove Thomas. The report of the board of inquiry, which hinted at faulty wiring as the cause of the disaster, dryly described the warden's hurried departure from the prison grounds during the fire and pointed out the lack of preparation for such an event, but at its conclusion the board withheld accusations. "At whose feet this negligence is to be laid is a matter of administration, and, therefore, in this final report, we make no recommendation thereon," the board's final report stated.[8] Despite widespread criticism of Thomas, several civic and prison groups came to the aid of the warden, and he returned to his post.

Thomas continued to serve as warden with repaired facilities but unchanged routines. In 1935, however, he was suspended by Governor Marin L. Davey after inmates testified that Thomas, his wife Mary, and son Donald had pampered a gangster ringleader of the bloodthirsty Purple Gang and retaliated against whistleblowers. Thomas, his wife, and son were removed from their living quarters and moved to a lakeside vacation cabin near his hometown in western Ohio, but in a few months, he was reinstated.[9] Thomas submitted his resignation a week later. For the rest of his life he worked in real estate, out of the public eye and unrepentant, until he died in Columbus, Ohio, after a year-long illness, the evening of October 5, 1952, at the age of eighty. He was survived by his wife, daughter Amanda, and son Donald, who had become a judge in Dayton, Ohio.[10]

Happy-go-lucky roads expert Raymond Beck lived a rather melancholic life after his service as chief engineer with the federal Council of National Defense. He returned to his job as head of the B. F. Goodrich Touring Bureau in 1919,[11] but left that position in 1921 to become head of the Cleveland Automobile Club, where he published a touring guide, *Auto Routes of Ohio*.[12] The following year, however, Beck's relationship with the Cleveland club soured. As an original member of the American Automobile Association (AAA), the Cleveland club was in Beck's sights when he targeted the AAA for being backed by commercial interests, "in a rut, self-centered and inefficient."[13] Always a rabble-rouser when it came to the automobiles using the nation's roads, Beck walked out of the AAA's 1922 St. Louis convention and helped form a rival, the National Automobile Association.

Beck's own efficiency was called into question in 1923, when his name was included in legal documents alleging copyright violations. The Automobile Blue Book, Inc., another early publisher of route information, claimed that the Goodrich Touring Bureau had filched its information,[14] but the case never went to court. At the time Beck lived in a rented home in Akron with his wife, Jennie, and a niece, but before 1930 they moved back to New Jersey, his home state, where he managed the Bergen County auto

Winners and Losers

club. He also continued a connection with northeast Ohio, advertising himself as "agent" for National Touring Bureaus, Inc. In reality, it was an insurance firm offering travel and pedestrian insurance, bail bond for motor vehicle miscreants, maps, and discounts on auto repairs.[15] Beck's residence remained in Bergen County, New Jersey, until his death in July 1954.

Governor James M. Cox campaigned unabashedly as a "war governor" in the fall of 1918, and when he won, he became Ohio's first three-term chief executive. His victory came despite opposition from Ohio's sizable German American population, which disliked Cox's support of President Wilson's anti-German policies; Cox in turn viewed his state's German population with suspicion, and one of his first acts after the war began was to confront "the danger of teaching German to our children in grade schools."[16] At the same time the influenza scourge exposed Ohio's inefficient health system, so in typical Progressive style he shepherded through the legislature a plan for urban health districts with full-time administrators. Postwar unemployment among returning war veterans also troubled Ohio, and Cox dealt with these by providing state funds for local infrastructure improvements that channeled jobs to veterans, although a flawed Ohio Labor Exchange registration process "discriminated against Negroes and other recent arrivals in the state or community," biographer Cebula notes. Cox observed that "Practically all the colored population in Ohio is resident in the cities,"[17] so the governor promoted Wilberforce College, a historically Black institution, as an agricultural alternative to city life for young African Americans. Cox also moved to reduce housing scarcity in Columbus by promoting construction of new dorms at Ohio State University to draw young people away from city life. In addition, he successfully dealt with postwar labor troubles across the state, encouraged funding for highway maintenance, and boasted that the state's reforms, including prison reform, had proved successful in his view.

When Cox was reelected in 1918, "he automatically became Democratic presidential material."[18] In early 1920, party executives met with him at Trailsend, his new mansion overlooking the Miami River valley five miles south of Dayton, and invited him to attend the July 1920, Democratic National Convention in San Francisco. He declined, insisting that anyone who might be a candidate should not appear in person, and subsequently his name was put into nomination against front-running candidates William G. McAdoo and A. Mitchell Palmer. After the first dozen ballots the Cox name inched close to the top of the ticket, but still short of the required two-thirds majority, until on the forty-fourth ballot Cox emerged as victor; a day later he tapped Franklin Delano Roosevelt, the assistant secretary of the navy, as his choice for vice-presidential candidate.

Cox vigorously supported the League of Nations, the worldwide effort to mold peaceful coexistence among nations that had arisen from the Versailles armistice talks. In contrast, his Republican opponent, Warren G. Harding, carefully avoided firm statements on policy in his campaign, which he conducted largely from the front porch of his home in Marion, Ohio. The two opponents, Cox and Harding, shared more than their native state: in the first and only presidential campaign of its kind, both candidates were newspaper publishers.

While the Republican stayed home, Democrat Cox immediately boarded a train for a tour of western states. The trip coursed through twenty-four states and featured 238 speeches. "This was a tremendously laborious and fatiguing ordeal," Cox complained later.[19] He found varying degrees of support: in Montana, the radical International Workers of the World, better known as the IWW or the "Wobblies," fell into grudging respect when they heard of Ohio's successful workmen's compensation law; in the Northwest, Cox encountered hecklers dispatched by Republican Chairman Will Hays (who in a few years would become the chief censor for the motion picture industry), and across the country the Cox organization, which traveled by rail, learned to recognize which party railroad crews favored. At campaign stops, nearby switching yard locomotives either hissed quietly in the background or huffed noisily during his speeches.

As the campaign progressed toward Election Day national Democrats counted opposition from many groups. German Americans opposed Wilson's legacy, which included refusal to recognize an Irish state, thus also infuriating the Irish. Black voters solidly supported the GOP because of the Democrats' saturation of the racist, segregated South, and despite Cox support for women's right to vote, Republicans claimed that American membership in the League of Nations would draw American soldiers back into international conflicts, a distressing possibility for American families.

Ultimately, Cox could not overcome Harding's simple call for a "Return to Normalcy." Voting revealed a substantial victory for the

Winners and Losers

Republican candidate, 60 percent to 34 percent and 404 electoral votes to 127 for Cox. Letters and telegrams poured into Trailsend to assure Cox that he had run a strong campaign, but Cox himself expressed no dismay. He foresaw problems ahead for the new president, and commented "in the circumstances, defeat had no sting for me."[20]

Troubles related to Harding's relationship with a group of corrupt supporters, the so-called "Ohio Gang," engulfed the Republican's presidency. With GOP scandal stories filling his newspaper's pages, Cox was proved prescient: in one incident, a humorist joked about the 1920 election. "My response was that I could easily understand how a humorist had been moved to such a joke," Cox wrote. "But I thought that the country now knew that as things had turned out the joke was not on me but on the country."[21]

The result of the 1920 election released Cox from politics to return to his real love, running newspapers as a wealthy publisher. In 1923 he visited Miami, Florida, and became enamored enough with the place that he purchased both land for a homestead there and then a Miami newspaper, the *Metropolis*, which he renamed the *Daily News*. When he returned to Ohio, he also bought the Canton *News*. With a new, crusading editor, Don Mellet, that paper began a battle against organized crime that helped improve its circulation until Mellet was assassinated in 1926. The paper subsequently won the Pulitzer Prize for Public Service, but without Mellet's leadership the *News* fell into decline, and Cox accepted an offer to sell the publication to its Canton rival, the *Repository*. Then Cox turned south again, buying the Atlanta *Journal*, with its fifty-thousand-watt radio station, WSB, in 1939.

Cox now found himself traveling over a newspaper and broadcast empire that stretched from Dayton in the north to Miami in the south. In his memoirs, he claimed that he didn't intend to build a centralized journalism empire: "Each journal was encouraged to maintain its own personality under its own staff,"[22] he wrote, a strategy echoed by Agnes Ash, one of his editors in Dayton and Atlanta. "He was very good [about local editorial management]. He let people running the paper run it," she said.[23]

Employees knew Cox as "a hard taskmaster, but he always had the welfare of his employees at heart," said Robert Snyder, an executive in the Cox organization.[24] Ash remembers that he traveled a lot, but when he was in town Cox made it a point to walk through the newsroom every day. "He was very polite, gracious, with formal manners," Ash said, "a very colorful man." He liked to wear trim suits imported from Britain, but "he was not a stiff," she noted. "He made an effort to be friendly. He would come through the newsroom and greet the women, mostly, calling them 'sister,' or 'sis,' or when they were older, 'mother.'"

"I always want the women who work for me to be comfortable," he told Ash. To encourage this, he had a cafeteria for women only installed on the fifth floor of the Dayton *Daily News* building, much to the chagrin of the male employees. The place served inexpensive food day and night, so the female employees who helped produce both morning and evening newspapers wouldn't need to visit bars for meals.[25]

"Cox told me he was very proud of working for women's rights when he was governor," Ash commented. On the other hand, women in the Cox editorial world toiled in the women's section only: Mary McCarty, a writer for the Cox organization whose mother worked for Cox as a women's section editor, said he followed the norms of his time. "He didn't rock the boat in significant ways," she said.

For example, Cox could be paternalistic with his newspaper families. McCarty said her mother, Vera Seiler McCarty, enjoyed working for Cox in the early 1950s even though he showed he could be guilty of micromanaging. On one occasion Vera and a newspaper friend had tickets to an Ohio State football game in Columbus, with her husband planning to chauffeur them the seventy miles to Ohio Stadium. But first, Cox himself called the McCarty household. "He wanted to know if the guy driving 'his girls' was a safe driver," Mary McCarty said.[26]

Cox continued to attend to his newspaper until his last days. He was in a meeting at the *Dayton Daily News*, as was typical, the day he dropped to his knees in the first in a series of strokes. His dire condition stunned his staff; "He was a presence," Ash said. Cox died July 15, 1957, at the age of eighty-seven, in his Trailsend mansion.

Epilogue

A MONTH AFTER James M. Cox died the official interstate route numbering map added Interstate 70—the planned replacement for US Route 40, the National Road. President Dwight Eisenhower, who had seen the efficient German autobahns during World War II, encouraged the creation of the national interstate highway system, which took on his name as the Dwight D. Eisenhower National System of Interstate and Defense Highways. Its construction was authorized by the Federal Aid Highway Act of 1956, and work began at several points in the nation that year. I-70 became the main east–west route across the country, in its eastern half following closely parallel to, and often consuming, the pavement of the National Road.

I-70's construction dragged the National Road in a full circle back to its old status as an all-but-forgotten secondary road. Yet before its importance faded, the Road served as one of the nation's premier highways, linking the nation's nineteenth-century dirt-road past with its four-lane twentieth-century future. The Pike's national importance to modern transportation was recognized as early as 1911, when the National Society of the Daughters of the American Revolution created the National Old Trails Road Committee. Chaired by Missouri judge and future US president Harry Truman, the private organization formally linked a series of quality roadways across the country. In 1912 the National Old Trails Road Association designated its route across the country, a 3,600-mile assemblage of good roads that included the National Road, as the National Old Trails Road, officially designated by red, white, and blue bands on signposts.

By the middle part of the twentieth century the National Road had arisen, phoenix-like, from a dusty, rutted farm path to a flourishing commercial artery. Today that culture is gone, too. Travelers on Route 40 now can see hundreds of shuttered tourist lodges, with weedy parking spaces and forlorn "no vacancy" signs; closed ice cream stands in tiny roadside settlements of a few gray wood houses at lonely crossroads; and the remains of antique gas stations with rusty, old-fashioned pumps once operated by "grease monkeys" whose mechanical work would be interrupted by a bell announcing the arrival of customers.

Travelers on Route 40 also can see seventeen-ton, eighteen-foot granite testimonials to the personalities who built "The Road That Helped Build the Nation." Twelve Madonna of the Trail statues were placed on the route, one in every state traversed by the National Road, by the Daughters of the American Revolution. Nominally, they honor the women who supported westward movement of white settlers in America, but in a practical sense the granite statues of a woman grasping a rifle in one hand while holding a child in the other honor Ebenezer Zane, Albert Gallatin, Logan Page, and the scores of engineers, visionaries, and politicians who pushed the National Road across the country. Harry Truman, as president of the National Old Trails Association, dedicated the first of these statues in 1928 in Springfield, Ohio, about sixty miles west of the point where Zane's Trace branched off the original National Road path. All the monuments have been maintained in good condition and are open to the public.

The man who spurred the National Road's reconstruction from a rutted dirt path to a paved roadway, Ohio Governor James M. Cox, is today recognized on a plaque in a tiny, preserved section of original pavement just west of New Concord, Ohio, where he placed the final brick of the massive undertaking. Aside from that honor, the mention of the Cox name as politician pales today in comparison to his renown as a businessman, for the name Cox is everywhere his media empire broadcasts or publishes its content.

On the other hand, history has lost the names of those who did much of the hard labor on the National Road. Contemporary reports and dignitaries at the closing ceremonies praised the toil, dedication, and patriotism of the more than three hundred convict workers, almost all African American, and many earned their release from prison. Yet no records formally link any prisoners' names to the project, save a dozen scrawled

Epilogue

notations indicating those who walked away. No enduring testament honors the convict laborers who hammered limestone to gravel, moved tons of sand by wheelbarrow, and carted the millions of blocks that became the pavement of the National Road.

Acknowledgments

JAMES MIDDLETON COX artifacts have surrounded me for my entire life. As a native of Dayton, Ohio, I see his name on the airport, the newspaper publishing company, and a television and radio broadcasting outlet. I've attended social events in his mansion and visited his family's resting place a few blocks from my present home. I had long considered writing his biography, but early in my research I discovered an interesting segment of his life that became this book. Digging through old files became a major task, and as the endeavor continued, it wove a net that ensnared a large number of people whose generosity needs to be recognized.

First and foremost is my wife, Karin, who deserves more than I have to offer for her years of tolerating my single-minded pursuit of minutiae about the National Road. This book belongs to you.

Next, I owe much to the Rev. Jack Smith of Deming, New Mexico, whose research skills corrected my misconceptions and filled a huge gap in the story of motoring pioneer Raymond Beck. That story likewise would not have evolved without the great help of The University of Akron Archival Services and Library Senior Associate John Ball.

Archivists enabled this book. The crew of the Ohio History Connection Archives and Library made invaluable resources available on an almost weekly basis. They offered suggestions, conducted searches, and at my request hauled weighty boxes down from storage. I can name Jenni Salamon, Lily Birkhimer, Kevin Latta, and Tom Rieder, but many others toiled namelessly for me.

At the Wright State University Special Collections and Archives, its former head, my friend and former colleague Dawne Dewey, opened a trove of documents that revealed background details about Governor Cox.

Acknowledgments

I believe photos give this work depth. David Adair of Cambridge and Rick Booth of the staff of the Guernsey County Historical Society helped build the framework with valuable, rare images, and in Muskingum County, Jerry L. Thompson personally led me on a tour of existing brick road sites and then gave me photographs and access to the files of the National Road/Zane Grey Museum. Betsy Taylor shared lots of local lore relating to the National Road.

Jessica Cromer, archivist at the National Afro-American Museum and Cultural Center, advised me about Bertillon cards, and Cyndie Gerken, author of books on the National Road and former president of the Ohio National Road association, shared old photos, documents, and lots of advice. Esteemed newspaper columnist Mary McCarty relayed family memories of working in the Cox publishing empire, and led me to Agnes Ash, who worked as an editor for Cox.

Lastly, this project would not have moved beyond my curiosity without the guidance of the editorial staff at The University of Akron Press. My gratitude goes to University of Akron Press Director Jon Miller, who gave this book direction; to kind and tolerant Editor Thea Ledendecker; to the relentless Editorial & Design Coordinator Amy Freels; to Julia Gammon in Marketing; and to all the other UA Press staff members who made this book a reality. Thank you.

Notes

FOREWORD

1. Betsy Taylor, interview, March 31, 2017.

NOTES ABOUT THE IMAGES

1. Wayne E. Fuller, "The Ohio Road Experiment 1913–1916," *Ohio History*, Winter 1965, 15.

2. "First Road Building by Prisoners in Ohio," Columbus *Sunday Dispatch*, September 29, 1912, 13.

INTRODUCTION

1. "Cox to Hurry Completion of National Road as Emergency War Step; Will Use Prisoners," *Ohio State Journal*, March 14, 1918, 2.

2. "Governor Cox Urges Hearty Cooperation in Road Building," *Daily Jeffersonian*, March 13, 1918, 1, 8.

3. "Governor Cox Urges Hearty Cooperation," 1, 8.

4. "Work Is Started Here and at Concord," Zanesville *Signal*, March 14, 1918, 1.

5. *Seventh Annual Report of the Ohio Board of Administration*, "The Ohio Penitentiary," June 30, 1918, 281.

6. Ohio State Penitentiary records show that African American men in the prison were incarcerated for crimes including murder, larceny, robbery, burglary, shooting or stabbing to wound, fraud and the like.

CHAPTER I

1. Jack Wills and Ebenezer Zane. e-WV: *The West Virginia Encyclopedia*, December 9, 2015, accessed August 2, 2020; Charles Wiseman, *Pioneer Period and Pioneer People of Fairfield County, Ohio* (Columbus, Ohio: F. J. Heer Printing Company, 1901), 11.

2. Zane Grey, Betty Zane. http://www.gutenberg.org, ch. XIV.

3. "To James Madison from Ebenezer Zane, 17 November 1795," *Founders Online*, National Archives, https://founders.archives.gov/documents/Madison/01-16-02-0069.

4. Rickie Longfellow, "Back in Time: Zane's Trace," *Highway History*, US Department of Transportation, Federal Highway Administration, https://www.fhwa.dot.gov/infrastructure/back0803.cfm, accessed August 28, 2018.

102

Notes   103

5. Glenn Harper and Doug Smith, *The Historic National Road in Ohio* (Springfield, Ohio, The Ohio National Road Association, 2010), 4.

6. Archer Butler Hulbert, *The Cumberland Road* (Cleveland, Ohio: Arthur H. Clark Company, 1904), 72.

7. Hulbert, *Cumberland*, 119–120.

8. *History of the Ohio Canals* (Columbus: Ohio State Archeological and Historical Society, 1905), 13.

9. Hulbert, *Cumberland*, 88.

10. "Interurban Railroads," *Ohio History Central*, https://ohiohistorycentral.org/w/Interurban_Railroads, accessed December 5, 2018.

11. See map of Midwest interurban lines, *Electric Railway Journal* (New York: McGraw Hill Publishing Company, 1908), 942.

12. Hulbert, *Cumberland*, 85–86.

13. Hulbert, *Cumberland*, 96.

14. Hulbert, *Cumberland*, 114.

15. Hulbert, *Cumberland*, 105.

16. Wayne E. Fuller, "The Ohio Road Experiment, 1913–1916," *Ohio History* 74, no. 1 (Winter 1965): 18.

CHAPTER II

1. "Just At the Close," *The Scioto Gazette*, Nov. 5, 1906, 3.

2. Albert Douglas, "Auto Trip Over the Old National Road," *Ohio Archaeological and Historical Publications*, vol. XVIII, 506.

3. "Douglas Says Not in Beverly But Columbus," *The Scioto Gazette*, July 18, 1910, 1.

4. "Douglas Says," 1.

5. Douglas, "Auto Trip," 504.

6. Douglas, "Auto Trip," 508.

7. Douglas, "Auto Trip," 512.

8. Craig E. Colten, "Adapting the Road to New Transportation Technologies," in *The National Road*, ed. Karl Raitz, 211.

9. Douglas, "Auto Trip," 504.

10. James M. Cox, *Journey Through My Years* (Macon, Georgia: Mercer University Press, 2004), 64. Reprinted from the 1948 edition by Simon & Schuster.

11. Cox, *Journey*, 58.

12. Cox, *Journey*, 116.

13. Roger B. Babson, "Boyhood Days: Cox's Family," in *Cox–the Man* (New York: Brentano's, 1920).

14. Cox, *Journey*, 12.

15. Cox, *Journey*, 14.

16. Cox, *Journey*, 15

17. Babson, "Goes to Cincinnati."

18. Cox, *Journey*, 25.

19. Cox, *Journey*, 25.

20. Cox, *Journey*, 34.

21. Cox, *Journey*, 38.

22. Babson, "Buys Dayton News," in *Cox–the Man*.

23. *Dayton Ink: The First Century of the Dayton Daily News* (Dayton, Ohio: *Dayton Daily News*, 1998), 6.

24. Cox, *Journey*, 43–49.

25. Cox, *Journey*, 57.

26. "Cox, the Man" in Morris, Charles E., *The Progressive Democracy of James M. Cox*. Indianapolis: The Bobbs-Merrill company, 1920.

27. Cox, *Journey*, 58.

28. Babson, "Congressional Campaign," in *Cox-the Man*.

29. Robert Bruce Graham. "James M. Cox and the Reform Movement in Ohio" (master's thesis, The Ohio State University, 1935), 10.

30. Cox, *Journey*, 116.

31. Cox, *Journey*, 130.

32. Babson, "Acquires a Springfield paper," in *Cox–the Man*.

33. Cox, *Journey*, 123.

34. Graham, "James M. Cox," 15.

35. Mitchel P. Roth, *Fire in the Big House* (Athens, Ohio: Swallow Press, 2019), Kindle.

36. "State motor vehicle registrations by years 1900–1995," http://www.fhwa.dot.gov, accessed January 7, 2021.

37. Wayne E. Fuller, "The Ohio Road Experiment 1913-1916," *Ohio History* 74, no. 1 (Winter 1965), 15.

38. Doris Kearns Goodwin. *The Bully Pulpit* (New York: Simon & Schuster, 2013), 574.

39. Fuller, "Ohio Road," 16.

40. Fuller, "Ohio Road," 16.

41. Fuller, "Ohio Road," 17.

42. Cox, *Journey*, 147.

43. Cox, *Journey*, 148.

44. Graham, "James M. Cox," 63.

45. Cox, *Journey*, 146.

46. Cox, *Journey*, 178.

CHAPTER III

1. Cox, *Journey*, 194.

Notes   105

2. Cox, *Journey*, 196.

3. "Akron Man Helps Plan Military Roads for Ohio," *Akron Beacon Journal*, April 25, 1917, 1.

4. Bruce E. Seely, *Building the American Highway System: Engineers as Policy Makers* (Philadelphia: Temple University Press, 1987), 43.

5. Testimony of E. C. Tibbetts in *Automobile Blue Book, Inc. v. The B. F. Goodrich Company*. Series VI, Public Relations Files, B. F. Goodrich Company Records, Archival Services, University Libraries, The University of Akron, Akron, Ohio.

6. Testimony of E. C. Tibbetts.

7. "A Tale of the Town," *Akron Beacon Journal*, March 30, 1917, 4.

8. "Promoting Interstate Road Through Summit Co. And Akron," *Akron Beacon Journal*, June 16, 1913, 1.

9. C. of C. Committee Outlines a Plan for Good Roads, *Akron Beacon Journal*, December 19, 1913, 18.

10. "High Cost of Living Due to Poor Roads," *Akron Beacon Journal*, October 31, 1914, 16.

11. "New Federal Aid Paving Will Benefit This City," *Akron Beacon Journal*, February 24, 1917, 13.

12. "Reese Fixes Truck Driver Who Wouldn't Let Him Pass," *Akron Beacon Journal*, March 21, 1917, 1.

13. March, Francis A. *History of the World War: An Authentic Narrative of the World's Greatest War* (Philadelphia: The United Publishers of the United States and Canada, 1919), 513.

14. Seely, *Building*, 24.

15. Seely, *Building*, 50.

16. "Official Correspondence Regarding the Requirements for Military Roads," *Better Roads and Streets* Magazine, July 1917, 314.

17. "Official Correspondence."

18. "To Improve Roads Despite the War," *Akron Beacon Journal*, September 24, 1917, 12.

19. "Akron Man to Make War Maps," Akron Beacon Journal, June 4, 1917, 11; "Goodrich Road Expert Is in The Service of Uncle Sam," *The Goodrich*, March 18, 1918, 9.

20. "Goodrich Road Expert."

21. "National Road at East City Limits Has Appearance of Being Shelled by Huns," *Cambridge Jeffersonian*, March 9, 1918, 1.

CHAPTER IV

1. "Cox, the Man," in Charles E. Morris, *The Progressive Democracy of James M. Cox*. 1920: Cox campaign literature.

2. "The East Pike Improvement is Declared to be War Emergency," Zanesville *Signal*, March 12, 1918, 1.

3. Agnes McCarty Ash, interview, May 23, 2019.

4. "Gov. Cox Here for A Road Conference," Zanesville *Signal,* March 12, 1; "Pike Improvement As War Measure Will Be Rushed—With Burton at Head," Zanesville *Signal,* March 13, 1918, 1.

5. Anthony Grasso, "Broken Beyond Repair: Rehabilitative Penology and American Political Development," *Political Research Quarterly 70,* vol. 2 (2017): 395–396.

6. Thomas Mott Osborne, *Society and Prisons* (New Haven: Yale University Press, 1916), 154.

7. Veronica Bagley, "Towards a Public History of the Ohio State Reformatory," honors thesis, The University of Akron, Spring 1918, 11–12.

8. Robert Bruce Graham, "James M. Cox and the Reform Movement in Ohio," master's thesis, The Ohio State University, 1935, 11.

9. Morris, "Cox, the Man," chapter VII.

10. "Convict Labor for Road Work," *Good Roads,* Nov. 24, 1917, 273; S. M. Williams, "The Honor System in the Use of Prison Labor in Construction and Maintenance of Public Highways," *Better Roads and Streets,* Vol. VII, No. 7, 1–2.

11. J. E. Clark, "Manufacture and Sales Departments Under the State Use System," *Ohio State Institution Journal* 3, No. 3 (January 1921): 33–46.

12. "State-Use System in Ohio," *Ninth Annual Report of the Ohio Board of Administration for the Fiscal Year Ended June 30, 1920, to the Governor of the State of Ohio,* 10.

13. Herbert J. Hovenkamp, "The Progressives: Racism and Public Law," *Faculty Scholarship* (2017): https://scholarship.law.upenn.edu/faculty_scholarship/1765/.

14. Ronald Takaki, *Iron Cages: Race and Culture in 19th Century America* (New York: Oxford University Press, 2000), 11.

15. Takaki, *Iron Cages, 13.*

16. United States Congress, "An Act to Establish an Uniform Rule of Naturalization" (March 26, 1790).

17. Pat Shipman, *The Evolution of Racism: Human Differences and the Use and Abuse of Science* (New York: Simon and Schuster, 1994), 102.

18. Shipman, *Evolution,* 128.

19. Douglas A. Blackmon, *Slavery by Another Name* (New York: Anchor Books, 2008), 240.

20. Woodrow Wilson, *A History of the American People,* vol. IX, Documentary Edition in Ten Volumes (New York: Harper & Brothers Publishers, 1902), 82.

21. Kathleen Wolgemuth, "Wilson and Federal Segregation," *The Journal of Negro History* 44, No. 2 (April 1959): 158–173, 162.

22. Morris, "Cox, the Man," chapter IV.

23. Ash, interview, May 23, 2019.

24. Cox, *Journey,* 216.

Notes 107

25. James E. Cebula, *James Cox: Journalist and Politician* (New York: Garland Publishing, 1985), 187.

CHAPTER V

1. "Cox to Hurry Completion of National Road as Emergency War Step; Will Use Prisoners," *Ohio State Journal*, March 14, 1918, 2.

2. "Prisoners Will Start Highway Work Next Week," Columbus *Evening Dispatch*, March 15, 1918, 15.

3. "Cox to Hurry," 2.

4. "Work Is Started on East Pike Here and At Concord," Zanesville *Signal*, March 14, 1918, 1.

5. "Cox to Hurry, 2"; "Tuesday to See National Road Work Under Way," Zanesville *Signal*, March 18, 1919, 1.

6. Mitchel P. Roth, *Fire in the Big House* (Athens, Ohio: Swallow Press, 2019), Kindle.

7. Roth, *Fire.*

8. James V. Bennett, *I Chose Prison* (New York: Alfred E. Knopf, 1970), 57.

9. All reports of the actions of the Ohio Highway Advisory Board are from its "*Director's Journal*," the official accounts of its weekly Tuesday meetings in 1918. The material quoted is from the March 19 meeting.

10. "Report Friday at Columbus on East Pike Proposals," Zanesville *Signal*, March 20, 1.

11. "Prisoners Will Do Half of Road Work and Contractors the Rest in Order to Speed War Plan," *Ohio State Journal*, March 20, 1918, 12.

12. "Woman on Job," Zanesville *Times Recorder*, June 6, 1918, 2.

13. Ohio Highway Advisory Board "*Director's Journal*," March 22, 1918.

14. "Local Men Can Work on East Pike and Help Win the War," Zanesville *Signal*, March 23, 1.

15. "Trucks to Start Within Two Weeks," *Columbus Evening Dispatch*, March 23, 1918, 5.

16. "U.S. Trucks Pass Through City," *Cambridge Jeffersonian*, May 9, 5; "Trucks Go Over Lincoln Highway," *Cambridge Jeffersonian*, May 11, 1.

17. "Warden Thomas Says He'll Ride Over Completed East Pike Fourth of July," Zanesville *Signal*, March 19, 1.

18. "Use of Prison Labor on Road Is Successful," *Columbus Evening Dispatch*, April 3, 1918, 3.

19. Cox, *Journey*, 156.

20. "Trusties at Pen Take Oath Before Leaving," *Columbus Evening Dispatch*, April 22, 1918, 6.

21. W. H. Alexander and C. A. Patton, "Ohio Weather for 1918," *Bulletin of the Ohio Agricultural Experiment Station*, Number 337, (June 1919), Wooster, Ohio.

22. Ohio Highway Advisory Board "Journal," May 17, 1918; Cox, *Journey*, 156.

23. Ohio Highway Advisory Board "Journal," May 21, 1918.

24. Ohio Highway Advisory Board "Journal," June 7, 1918.

25. Ohio Highway Advisory Board "Journal," June 7, 1918.

CHAPTER VI

1. "Over Three Hundred Prisoners Working," *Columbus Sunday Dispatch*, June 23, 1918, 14.

2. "Convicts on the Road," *Ohio State Journal*, April 5, 1918, 4.

3. "Use of Prison Labor on Road Is Successful," *Columbus Evening Dispatch*, April 3, 1918, 3.

4. *Journal of the Ohio Highway Advisory Board*, June 25, 1918.

5. "Paying for Road Work," *Ohio State Journal*, April 9, 1918, 4.

6. "103 State Prisoners Made Ill, Supposedly from Jelly," *Ohio State Journal*, March 30, 1918, 1; "It's the Grip at Pen, Not Poison," *Ohio State Journal*, April 3, 1918, 1.

7. "Convicts on the Road," *Ohio State Journal*, April 5, 1918, 4.

8. "Observations," *Columbus Evening Dispatch*, June 27, 1918, 4.

9. "Ministers To Meet," Zanesville *Times Recorder*, June 3, 1918, 7.

10. "East Pike Paving Project Began as Wartime Emergency Measure," Zanesville *Sunday Times Signal*, May 20, 1951, 8.

11. "Dr. Kellogg Visits Boys on East Pike," Zanesville *Times Recorder*, June 10, 1918, 7.

12. "Reformatory Men Doing Good Work on The East Pike," Zanesville *Times Recorder*, June 26, 1918, 8.

13. "Pike Workers in Shooting Affray," Zanesville *Times Recorder*, July 9, 1918, 1; "Victims of Shooting Not Out of Danger," July 10, 2.

14. "Ball Bat Wielder at Large," Zanesville *Times Recorder*, October 11, 1918, 12.

15. "Ohio Weather for 1918," 683.

16. Betsy Taylor, interview, March 21, 2017.

17. "Good Progress Is Now Being Made on East Pike Project," Zanesville *Times Recorder*, June 6, 1918, 1.

18. "To Care For Those on East Pike," Zanesville *Times Recorder*, April 27, 1918, 7.

19. "Armbrister, Sr., Is Badly Injured," Zanesville *Times Recorder*, June 19, 1918, 6.

20. "Has Foot Crushed," Zanesville *Times Recorder*, July 11, 1918, 2.

21. David Adair, interview, July 18, 2017.

22. *Journal of the Ohio Highway Advisory Board*, May 21, 1918.

23. "To Care For Those Hurt On The East Pike, Switch Sidings Located," Zanesville *Times Recorder*, April 27, 1918, p. 7.

24. *Journal*, August 14, 1918.

25. *Journal*, June 7, 1918.

Notes   109

26. Cox, *Journey*, 156. "Only one prisoner was guilty of an infraction of the rules of conduct," Cox recalled in his memoir. "He was caught by some of his fellows and pretty badly beaten up. They felt he had brought discredit to the whole group."

27. "Two More Prisoners Quit East Pike Work," Zanesville *Times Recorder*, June 6, 1918, 2.

28. "Police Make Big Bag of Alleged Draft Evaders," Zanesville *Times Recorder*, July 10, 1918, 6.

29. All production costs and estimates are from contracts and reports provided to the Highway Advisory Board during the spring and summer of 1918.

30. Richard Rothstein, *The Color of Law* (New York: Liveright Publishing Corporation, 2017), 155, Kindle.

31. "Ohio Paving Brick Men To Hold Meeting Here," Zanesville *Times Recorder*, July 13, 1918, 10.

32. *Journal*, July 23, 1918.

33. Cox, *Journey*, 156.

CHAPTER VII

1. "Warden Thomas Would Supervise Building Roads," *Columbus Sunday Dispatch*, September 1, 1918, 1.

2. "Governor Delivers Labor Day Address," Columbus Evening Dispatch, September 3, 1918, 6; "Cox Speaks Monday to Labor Day Workers," *Akron Beacon Journal*, September 3, 1918, 2.

3. "Trusties Are Favored," Columbus *Sunday Dispatch*, August 11, 1918, 11.

4. "Prisoners Make Good As Highway Builders," *Columbus Sunday Dispatch,* September 15, 1918, 12.

5. "Truck Trains to Pike In Future," Zanesville *Times Recorder*, July 27, 1918, 6.

6. "Badly Injured in Auto Wreck," *Columbus Evening Dispatch*, October 5, 1918, 1.

7. "Asks That Road be Improved, At Once," *Cambridge Daily Jeffersonian*, October 13, 1918, 1.

8. *Journal*, Oct. 21, 1918.

CHAPTER VIII

1. National Oceanic and Atmospheric Administration, https://www.noaa.gov/weather, accessed Sept. 19, 2019.

2. "Big Celebration Today to Mark Opening of Improved East Pike," Zanesville *Times Recorder*, October 22, 1918, 1, 3.

3. Detailed reports of the last-brick ceremonies were published on page one of both the Zanesville *Times Recorder* and the Cambridge *Daily Jeffersonian* for October 23, 1918.

4. "Imposing Ceremonies on Historic S Bridge," *Daily Jeffersonian*, October 23, 1918, 1.

5. "Imposing Were the Ceremonies," *Daily Jeffersonian*, Oct. 23, 1918, 8.

6. "Imposing," 8.

7. "Traffic Was Heavy," *Daily Jeffersonian*, October 28, 1918, 5.

8. "Usefulness of National Road Is Endangered," *Daily Jeffersonian*, October 30, 1918, 4.

9. "To Extend Mail Service Over National Road," *Daily Jeffersonian*, November 1, 1918, 4; "Motor Truck Mail Service on Pike," *Daily Jeffersonian*, November 5, 1918, 3.

10. "Army Truck Train Enroute East," *Daily Jeffersonian*, November 8, 1918, 5.

CHAPTER IX

1. National Oceanic and Atmospheric Administration, Record of Climatological Observations November and December 1918, https://www.ncdc.noaa.gov/cdo-web/, accessed September 25, 2019.

2. Correspondence between Acting Superintendent T. C. Jenkins and the Ohio Board of Administration, October–November 1918. Ohio History Connection, State Archives Series 832.

3. Merritt Ierley, *Traveling the National Road: Across the Centuries on America's First Highway* (Woodstock, New York: Overlook Press, 1990), 191.

4. Mrs. Henry D. Wiseman, "An Auto Trip by Five Ladies from Corydon, Indiana, Through the East," *The Hoosier Motorist*, August 1920, 23–24.

5. Wiseman, "Auto Trip," 24.

6. Philip D. Jordan, *The National Road* (Indianapolis: Bobbs-Merrill Company, 1948), 387.

7. Norris Schneider, *The National Road: Main Street of America* (Columbus, Ohio: Ohio Historical Society), 34.

8. Bruce E. Seely, *Building the American Highway System: Engineers as Policy Makers*, (Philadelphia: Temple University Press, 1987), 57.

9. Jordan, *The National Road*, 388.

10. Ierley, *Traveling*, 199.

11. Ierley, *Traveling*, 199.

12. Glenn Harper and Doug Smith, *The Historic National Road in Ohio* (Springfield: The Ohio National Road Association, 2010), 6.

13. Jordan, *The National Road*, 396.

CHAPTER X

1. *Journal of the Senate*, Eighty-third General Assembly of the State of Ohio, Vol. CVIII. Columbus, Ohio, F. J. Hess Printing Co., 1919, 1054–56.

2. Norris F. Schneider, "East Pike Paving Project Began as Wartime Emergency Measure," Zanesville *Sunday Times Signal*, May 20, 1951, 8.

3. F. Coker, "Dogmas of Administrative Reform: As Exemplified in the Recent Reorganization in Ohio." *American Political Science Review* 16, no. 3 (1922): 402.

Notes

4. "Rufus C. Burton, Retired Manufacturer and Capitalist, Is Taken by Death," Zanesville *Times Recorder*, June 15, 1928, 1.

5. Roth, *Fire*.

6. "Prisoners in Open Defiance of Guards; Death Toll Now 318," *Columbus Evening Dispatch,* April 23, 1930, 1.

7. "Prisoner Outlines Inmates' Passive Resistance Plans," *Columbus Evening Dispatch*, April 24, 1930, 1.

8. Attorney General Gilbert Bettman, et al., Ohio Penitentiary Fire Report, Ohio University Mahn Center for Archives & Special Collections, https://ohiomemory.org/digital/collection.

9. Roth, *Fire*.

10. "P. E. Thomas, Ex-Warden, Dies at 80," *Columbus Evening Dispatch*, October 6, 1952, 1.

11. "Automobile Club Represented at Road Conference," *Akron Beacon Journal*, January 18, 1919.

12. "Auto Routes of Ohio: New Touring Guide Published for Distribution to Members of Clubs," *Ohio Motorist*, June 1921, 16.

13. "Xtry! About the A.A.A.: Protest Against "Commercialism" Not Heeded at Convention, So New National Body Formed," *Motor West*, Vol. 37 (June 15, 1922), 36.

14. Testimony of E. C. Tibbetts in *Automobile Blue Book, Inc. v. The B. F. Goodrich Company*. Series VI, Public Relations Files, B. F. Goodrich Company Records, Archival Services, University Libraries, The University of Akron, Akron, Ohio.

15. "$10,012.25 for $3.50" advertising, *Akron Beacon Journal*, January 4, 1933, p. 22.

16. Cox, *Journey*, 212.

17. James E. Cebula, *James Cox: Journalist and Politician* (New York: Garland Publishing, 1985), 227.

18. Cebula, 221.

19. Cox, *Journey,* 267.

20. Cox, *Journey*, 284.

21. Cox, *Journey*, 285.

22. Cox, *Journey*, 392.

23. Agnes McCarty Ash, interview, May 23, 2019.

24. "On James M. Cox," in *Dayton Ink: The First Century of the Dayton Daily News. Dayton Daily News*, Dayton, Ohio, 1998, 43.

25. "The Demise of the Women's Cafeteria," *Dayton Ink*, 44.

26. Mary McCarty, interview, April 23, 2019.

Bibliography

SOURCES REGARDING THE NATIONAL ROAD AND ITS HISTORY

1916 Atlas. Guernsey County Map Department, https://www.guernseycountymaps.org/maps/historical-atlas-and-plats.

Adair, David. Interview. August 2, 2018.

Beers, F. W. *Atlas of Muskingum County Ohio*. New York: Beers, Soule and Co., 1866. Ohio History Connection Archives and Library.

Colten, Craig E. "Adapting the Road to New Transportation Technologies." In *The National Road,* edited by Karl Raitz, Baltimore: Johns Hopkins Press, 1996.

Grant, H. Roger. *Ohio on the Move*. Athens: Ohio University Press, 2000.

Grey, Zane. *Betty Zane*. https://www.gutenberg.org/ebooks/1261.

Harper, Glenn, and Doug Smith. *The Historic National Road in Ohio*. Springfield: The Ohio National Road Association, 2010.

History of the Ohio Canals. Columbus: The Ohio State Archeological and Historical Society, 1905, 13.

Hulbert, Archer Butler. *The Cumberland Road*. Cleveland, Ohio: The Arthur H. Clark Company, 1904.

Ierley, Merritt. *Traveling the National Road: Across the Centuries on America's First Highway*. Woodstock, New York: Overlook Press, 1990.

Jordan, Philip D. *The National Road*, Indianapolis: Bobbs-Merrill Company, 1948.

Longfellow, Rickie. "Back in Time: Zane's Trace." In *Highway History*, US Department of Transportation, Federal Highway Administration. Accessed August 28, 2018. https://www.fhwa.dot.gov/infrastructure/back0803.cfm.

Muskingum County, Ohio, Engineer's Office, *1915 Tax Maps*. http://www.mceo.org/scans/Tax%20Maps/tax%20maps%201915/muskingum%20township/.

Bibliography 113

Schneider, Norris F. *The National Road: Main Street of America.* Columbus: The Ohio Historical Society, 1975.

Seely, Bruce E. *Building the American Highway System: Engineers as Policy Makers.* Philadelphia: Temple University Press, 1987.

Thompson, Jerry. Interview. June 27, 2018.

Wiseman, Charles. *Pioneer Period and Pioneer People of Fairfield County, Ohio.* Columbus, Ohio: F. J. Heer Printing Company, 1901.

JAMES M. COX BIOGRAPHY AND SOURCES

Ash, Agnes McCarty. Interview. May 23, 2019.

Babson, Roger B. *Cox–the Man.* New York: Brentano's, 1920.

Cebula, James E. *James Cox: Journalist and Politician.* New York: Garland Publishing, 1985.

Cox, James M. *Journey Through My Years.* Macon, Georgia: Mercer University Press, 2004. Reprinted from the 1948 edition by Simon & Schuster.

Dayton Ink: The First Century of the Dayton Daily News. Dayton Daily News, 1998.

Graham, Robert Bruce. "James M. Cox and the Reform Movement in Ohio." Master's thesis, The Ohio State University, 1935.

James M. Cox Papers. Wright State University Special Collections and Archives, Collection Number MS-2, Box 5.

McCarty, Mary. Interview. April 23, 2019.

Morris, Charles E. "Cox, the Man." In *The Progressive Democracy of James M. Cox.* Cox campaign literature, 1920.

SOURCES REGARDING PRISONS, PRISONERS, AND PRISON LABOR ON THE NATIONAL ROAD PROJECT

"103 State Prisoners Made Ill, Supposedly from Jelly." *Ohio State Journal.* March 30, 1918.

Bagley, Veronica. "Towards a Public History of the Ohio State Reformatory." Honors thesis, The University of Akron, Spring 1918, 11–12.

"Ball Bat Wielder At Large." Zanesville *Times Recorder*, October 11, 1918, 12.

Bennett, James V. *I Chose Prison.* New York: Alfred E. Knopf, 1970.

Bertillon cards with photographs, 1901–1921, Ohio State Reformatory. Ohio History Connection, State Archives Series 1416AV, Box 4031–4033.

———. 1888–1919, Ohio Penitentiary. Ohio History Connection, State Archives Series 1002AV.

Blackmon, Douglas A. *Slavery by Another Name.* New York: Anchor Books, 2008.

Clark, J. E. "Manufacture and Sales Departments Under the State Use System," *The Ohio State Institution Journal* 3, no. 3 (January 1921): 33–46.

"Convict Labor for Road Work." *Good Roads.* Nov. 24, 1917.

"Convicts on the Road." *Ohio State Journal.* April 5, 1918, 4.

"Cox to Hurry Completion of National Road as Emergency War Step; Will Use Prisoners." *Ohio State Journal.* March 14, 1918, 2.

Darby, Nancy K. *The Ohio State Reformatory.* Charleston, South Carolina: Arcadia Publishing, 2016.

"Four Youths Escape," *Columbus Evening Dispatch* June 8, 1918, 7.

Grasso, Anthony. "Broken Beyond Repair: Rehabilitative Penology and American Political Development," *Political Research Quarterly* 70, no. 2 (2017): 395–396.

Index to registry of prisoners, 1913–1957. Ohio Penitentiary. Ohio History Connection, State Archives Series 2692, BV7729.

"It's the Grip at Pen, Not Poison." *Ohio State Journal.* April 3, 1918, 1.

Jenkins, Thomas C. Correspondence with the Ohio Board of Administration, October–November 1918. Ohio History Connection Archives.

"Dr. Kellogg Visits Boys on East Pike." Zanesville *Times Recorder,* June 10, 1918, 7.

Meyers, David, Elise Meyers Walker and James Dailey II. *Inside the Ohio Penitentiary.* Charleston, South Carolina: The History Press, 2013.

Ohio Penitentiary Register of Prisoners, Ohio History Connection Archives/ Library, Series 2692.

Ohio State Reformatory. Record of Inmates, 1918–1954 (microfilm). Ohio History Connection, State Archives Series 1721, reels GR3606–3607.

"Over Three Hundred Prisoners Working." *Columbus Sunday Dispatch*, June 23, 1918, 14.

Osborne, Thomas Mott. *Society and Prisons.* New Haven: Yale University Press, 1916.

"Pen Convicts To Do Pike Work In This County Now," Zanesville *Times Recorder.* May 16, 1918, 10.

"East Pike Work Done By 307 Of State Charges," Zanesville *Times Recorder,* June 24, 1918, 3.

"For Pike Employes," Zanesville *Times Recorder* June 4, 1918, 7.

"Pike Workers in Shooting Affray." Zanesville *Times Recorder.* July 9, 1918, 1.

"Police Make Big Bag of Alleged Draft Evaders," Zanesville *Times Recorder.* July 10, 1918, 6.

"Prisoners in Open Defiance of Guards; Death Toll Now 318." *Columbus Evening Dispatch*, April 23, 1930, 1.

"Prisoners Make Good As Highway Builders." *Columbus Sunday Dispatch,* September 15, 1918, 12.

Bibliography 115

"Prisoners Will Do Half of Road Work and Contractors the Rest in Order to Speed War Plan." *Ohio State Journal.* March 20, 1918, 12.

Record of Escaped Prisoners, 1834–1935. Ohio History Connection, State Archives Series 1363, BV7014.

"Reformatory Boys Have Lively Game," Zanesville *Times Recorder,* June 13, 1918, 8.

"Reformatory Inmates At Work On East Pike," Zanesville *Times Recorder,* May 28, 19182.

"Reformatory Men Doing Good Work on The East Pike," Zanesville *Times Recorder,* June 26, 1918, p. 8.

Roth, Mitchel P. *Fire in the Big House* (Kindle ed.). Athens, Ohio: Swallow Press, 2019.

Rothstein, Richard. *The Color of Law* (Kindle ed.), 2017. New York: Liveright Publishing Corporation.

Seventh Annual Report of the Ohio Board of Administration, "The Ohio Penitentiary," June 30, 1918. p. 281.

"State-Use System in Ohio," *Ninth Annual Report of the Ohio Board of Administration for the Fiscal Year Ended June 30, 1920,* to the Governor of the State of Ohio, 10.

Takaki, Ronald. *Iron Cages: Race and Culture in 19th Century America.* New York: Oxford University Press, 2000.

"Trusties Are Favored." *Columbus Sunday Dispatch,* August 11, 1918, 11.

"Trusties at Pen Take Oath Before Leaving." *Columbus Evening Dispatch,* April 22, 1918, 6.

"Two More Prisoners Quit East Pike Work," Zanesville *Times Recorder,* June 6, 1918, 2.

"Warden Thomas Says He'll Ride Over Completed East Pike Fourth of July," Zanesville *Signal,* March 19, 1.

"Warden Thomas Would Supervise Building Roads," *Columbus Sunday Dispatch,* September 1, 1918, p. 1.

"Work Is Started Here and at Concord," Zanesville *Signal,* March 14, 1918, p. 1.

ROAD CONSTRUCTION AND MISCELLANEOUS SUBJECT MATTER SOURCES

"Armbrister, Sr. Is Badly Injured," Zanesville *Times Recorder,* June 19, 1918, 6.

"Automobile Club Represented at Road Conference," *Akron Beacon Journal,* January 18, 1919.

"A Tale of the Town." *Akron Beacon Journal* March 30, 1917, 4.

"Army Truck Train Enroute East." *The Daily Jeffersonian,* November 8, 1918, 5.

"Asks That Road be Improved, At Once." *The Daily Jeffersonian*, October 13, 1918, 1.

"Auto Routes of Ohio: New touring guide published for distribution to members of clubs." *Ohio Motorist*, June 1921, 16.

Automobile Blue Book, Inc. v. The B. F. Goodrich Company. Testimony of E. C. Tibbetts. Series VI, Public Relations Files, B. F. Goodrich Company Records, Archival Services, University Libraries, The University of Akron, Akron, Ohio.

"Badly Injured in Auto Wreck." *Columbus Evening Dispatch*, October 5, 1918, 1.

Bettman, Gilbert, et al. *Ohio Penitentiary Fire Report*, Ohio University Mahn Center for Archives & Special Collections, https://ohiomemory.org/digital/collection/p267401coll36/id/15939/rec/1.

"Big Celebration Today to Mark Opening of Improved East Pike," Zanesville *Times Recorder*, October 22, 1918, p. 1, p. 3.

"C. Of C. Committee Outlines a Plan for Good Roads." *Akron Beacon Journal*, December 19, 1913, p. 18.

Coker, F. "Dogmas of Administrative Reform: As Exemplified in the Recent Reorganization in Ohio." *American Political Science Review* 16, no. 3 (1922): 399–411.

"Cox Speaks Monday to Labor Day Workers." *Akron Beacon Journal*, September 3, 1918.

Director's Journal, 1917–1972. Ohio Department of Highways, 1918. Ohio History Connection, State Archives Series 4126, BV 6783.

Douglas, Albert. "Auto Trip Over the Old National Road." In *Ohio Archaeological and Historical Publications*, Vol. XVIII, 506.

"Douglas Says Not in Beverly But Columbus." *Scioto Gazette*, July 18, 1910.

"East Pike Paving Being Pushed to Early Completion," Zanesville *Times Recorder*, July 19, 1918, 5.

Fuller, Wayne E. "The Ohio Road Experiment, 1913–1916." *Ohio History* 74, no. 1 (Winter 1965): 18.

Goodwin, Doris Kearns. *The Bully Pulpit*. New York: Simon & Schuster, 2013.

"Governor Cox Urges Hearty Cooperation in Road Building." *The Daily Jeffersonian*, March 13, 1918, 1, 8.

"Governor Delivers Labor Day Address." *Columbus Evening Dispatch*, September 3, 1918, 6.

"High Cost of Living Due to Poor Roads." *Akron Beacon Journal*, October 31, 1914, 16.

Hovenkamp, Herbert J. "The Progressives: Racism and Public Law." (2017). Faculty Scholarship. https://scholarship.law.upenn.edu/faculty_scholarship/1765/.

Bibliography

"The Improved East Pike," Zanesville *Times Recorder*, October 22, 1918, 4.

"Improved East Pike To Be Opened For Traffic Next Monday Morning," Zanesville *Times Recorder,* October 12, 1918, p. 1.

"Interurban Railroads," Ohio History Central, https://ohiohistorycentral.org/w/Interurban_Railroads, accessed December 5, 2018.

Journal of the Senate, Eighty-third General Assembly of the State of Ohio, Vol. CVIII. Columbus, Ohio: The F. J. Hess Printing Co., 1919.

"Just at the close." *The Scioto Gazette* Nov. 5, 1906, 3

March, Francis A. *History of the World War: An authentic narrative of the World's greatest war*. Philadelphia: The United Publishers of the United States and Canada, 1919.

"Ministers To Meet," Zanesville *Times Recorder,* June 3, 1918, 7.

"Motor Truck Mail Service on Pike." *The Daily Jeffersonian*, November 5, 1918, p3.

Motor vehicle registrations, 1908–1912. Ohio Bureau of Motor Vehicles. Ohio History Connection, State Archives Series 4559.

"Must Detour To New Concord By Rix Mills Road," Zanesville *Times Recorder,* May 22, 1918, 2.

National Oceanic and Atmospheric Administration, *Record of Climatological Observations November and December 1918*. Accessed September 25, 2019, https://www.weather.gov/wrh/Climate?wfo=pbz

"National Road at East City Limits Has Appearance of Being Shelled by Huns," *Daily Jeffersonian*, March 9, 1918, 1.

"New Federal Aid Paving Will Benefit This City." *Akron Beacon Journal*, February 24, 1917, 13.

"Official Correspondence Regarding the Requirements for Military Roads." *Better Roads and Streets*, July 1917, 314.

Ohio Department of Transportation. Record of Contracts Let. (microfilm) Ohio History Connection, State Archives Series 2089, roll GR5176.

"Ohio Paving Brick Men To Hold Meeting Here," Zanesville *Times Recorder,* July 13, 1918, 10.

"P. E. Thomas, Ex-Warden, Dies at 80." *Columbus Evening Dispatch,* October 6, 1952, p. 1.

"Pike Improvement As War Measure Will Be Rushed–With Burton at Head" Zanesville *Signal*, March 13, 1918, p. 1.

"The East Pike Improvement is Declared to be War Emergency." Zanesville *Signal,* March 12, 1918, 1.

"Promoting Interstate Road Through Summit Co. And Akron." *Akron Beacon Journal*, June 16, 1913, p. 1.

"Reese fixes truck driver who wouldn't let him pass." *Akron Beacon Journal,* March 21, 1917, p. 1.

"Rufus C. Burton, Retired Manufacturer and Capitalist, Is Taken by Death," Zanesville *Times Recorder* June 15, 1928.

Schneider, Norris F. "East Pike Paving Project Began As Wartime Emergency Measure." Zanesville *Sunday Times Signal* May 20, 1951.

Shipman, Pat. *The Evolution of Racism: Human Differences and the Use and Abuse of Science.* New York: Simon and Schuster, 1994.

Taylor, Betsy. Interview, March 31, 2017.

Testimony of E. C. Tibbetts in *Automobile Blue Book, Inc. v. The B. F. Goodrich Company.* Series VI, Public Relations Files, B. F. Goodrich Company Records, Archival Services, University Libraries, The University of Akron, Akron, Ohio.

"To Care for Those Hurt on East Pike," Zanesville *Times Recorder,* April 27, 1918.

"To Extend Mail Service Over National Road." *Daily Jeffersonian,* November 1, 1918.

"To Improve Roads Despite the War." *Akron Beacon Journal* September 24, 1917, 12.

"Traffic Was Heavy." *Daily Jeffersonian,* October 28, 1918, 5.

"Trucks to Start Within Two Weeks." *Columbus Evening Dispatch,* March 23, 1918, 5.

"Truck Train to Pike In Future," Zanesville *Times Recorder,* July 27, 1918, 6.

United States Congress, "An act to establish an uniform Rule of Naturalization" (March 26, 1790).

"Use of Prison Labor on Road Is Successful." *Columbus Evening Dispatch,* April 3, 1918, 3.

"Usefulness of National Road Is Endangered," *Daily Jeffersonian,* October 30, 1918, 4.

"Victims of Shooting Not Out of Danger," Zanesville *Times Recorder,* July 11, 1918, 2.

W. H. Alexander and C. A. Patton, "Ohio Weather for 1918." *Bulletin of the Ohio Agricultural Experiment Station,* Number 337, (June 1919) Wooster, Ohio.

Williams, S. M. "The Honor System in the Use of Prison Labor in Construction and Maintenance of Public Highways." *Better Roads and Streets,* Vol. VII, No. 7, 1–2.

Wills, Jack. Ebenezer Zane. e-WV: *The West Virginia Encyclopedia.* Accessed 09 December 2015, 02 August 2020, https://www.wvencyclopedia.org/articles/1397.

Wilson, Woodrow. *A History of the American People,* Vol. IX (Documentary

Bibliography

Edition in Ten Volumes). New York: Harper & Brothers Publishers, 1902.

Wiseman, Mrs. Henry D. "An Auto Trip by Five Ladies from Corydon, Indiana, through the East," *The Hoosier Motorist*, August 1920, 23–24.

Wolgemuth, Kathleen. "Wilson and Federal Segregation," *The Journal of Negro History*, Vol. 44, No. 2 (April 1959), 158–173, 162.

"Xtry! About the A.A.A.: Protest Against 'Commercialism' Not Heeded at Convention, So New National Body Formed," *Motor West*, Vol. 37 (June 15, 1922), 36.

Index

Akron Beacon Journal, 30
Alsdorf, W. A., 28
Anti-Saloon League, 26
Archer, Charles, 81
Armbrister, Albert, Sr., 60
Ash, Agnes, 42, 95, 96
Atlanta Journal, 95
Automobile Blue Book, Inc., 83, 92
Ayers & Kappes (construction firm), 62, 88

B. F. Goodrich, 28–29, 33, 83, 92
Babson, Roger, 16, 17, 18
Baily, Albert, 81
Baker, Newton, 31–32
Baltimore & Ohio Railroad, 60, 73
Beck, Jennie, 92
Beck, Raymond, advocate for National
    Road renewal, 1, 31, 32–35; "borrowed"
    from Goodrich for war service, 32; as
    federal field engineer, 33, 39, 49, 51;
    with Goodrich Touring Bureau,
    29–30; meets with Governor Cox,
    27–28, 33, 35; postwar life, 92, 93; road
    map pioneer, 28–29, 83
Bell, Carrie, 41
Benz, Agnes, 47
Berek, Tony, 65
Bertillon, Alphonse, 39
Bertillon system, 39
Better Roads and Streets magazine, 37
Bishop, H. K., 47–48
Boyd, James, 58
Bridgeport, Ohio, 7
Brockway, Zebulon, 37
Brown, Arthur, 65
Bruning, Henry D., 62–63, 71
Bryan, William Jennings, 18, 23
Bureau of Public Roads, 84

Burton, Rufus C., on B&O railroad, 61–62;
    as contractor, 35–36, 46–48, 50, 52,
    68–69, 89–90; on convict labor, 51;
    hires medical service, 59; meets with
    Highway Board, 50–51, 70–71, 82;
    plans closing ceremony, 72, 75, 77;
    post-World War I life, 90
Burton-Townsend Brick Company, 35–36,
    46, 90
Butchers, C. B., 33
Butler, Lubin, 58

Cable, George Washington, 41
Cambridge, Ohio, 33, 35, 44, 50, 58–59, 61,
    71, 77–79, 101; grows with National
    Road, 8; speeded bricking requested,
    73; truck caravans pass through, 49,
    79; welcomes road project, 1, 36
Century Inn, 85
Chapin, Roy W., 32–33
Chillicothe, Ohio, 11, 12, 13, 28, 50, 56, 83
Circleville, Ohio, 89
Clarendon Hotel, 35, 75
Columbus, Ohio, 1, 28, 34, 35, 38, 43, 47, 50,
    68, 72, 75–76, 78, 85, 92–93, 96;
    National Road pavement destination,
    7–8, 25, 36, 86, 91; rail arrives, 9
Columbus Dispatch, 50, 65, 71, 91
Cooper, Myers, 91
Cornwallis, Charles, 5
Corydon, Indiana, 83
Council of National Defense, Ohio
    Branch, 1, 32, 35, 42, 92
Cowen, Clinton, 35, 46–47, 51–52, 54, 63,
    71, 73–74, 82, 90
Cox, Gilbert, 16
Cox, James Middleton, 1, 3, 15, 98; on
    convict labor, 37, 38, 50; death, 96–97;

120

Index   121

as House of Representatives member, 15–16, 20–22; loses to Willis, 26; and National Road project, 28, 31, 32–37, 44, 46–47, 51–54, 69, 71–72; as newspaper publisher, 19–21, 95, 96; as Ohio governor, 22–25; as presidential candidate, 93–95; on race relations, 42–43; re-elected, 27; 39, 75, 77–78, 87, 89, 91; youth, 16–18
Cox, Mayme Simpson, 21
Croxton, Fred, 43
Cumberland, Maryland, 83
Cumberland Pike. *See* National Road
Cumberland Road. *See* National Road
Curry, Will "Deacon", 81

Daily Jeffersonian newspaper, 78
Darwin, Charles, 39
Davey, Marin L., 92
Davis, Charles, 81
Dawson, Ira P., 79
Dayton, Ohio, 15, 20, 27, 65, 92–93, 95
Dayton Daily News, 19, 42, 96
Deacon, W. E., 76
Dennis, John, 81
Dixon, Thomas, 42
Dodd, Harriet Burton, 77
Donahey, Victor, 34–35, 52–53, 75
Douglas, Albert, Jr., 3, 11, 16, 23, 28, 33, 83; advocates better roads, 14–15; lengthy motor tour, 12; takes National Road tour, 13
Douglas, Albert, Sr., 11
Douglas, Lucia, 11–13

Eisenhower, Dwight D., 97
Elmira Reformatory, New York, 37
Eugenics Records Office, 41

Fawcett, W. C., 44
Federal Aid Highway Act of 1956, 97
Federal Highway Act of 1921, 84
Felton, Samuel M., 17
Ferguson & Edmondson, contractors, 55, 82
Fincastle, Fort. *See* Fort Henry
Firestone, Harvey, 43
Ford Model T, 83

Fort Henry, 4, 5
Fort Stanwix, Treaty of, 4
Fuller, Wayne E., 22–23

Gallatin, Albert, 6, 98
Garfield, James R., 26
George, Ella F., 90
Gheeter, John, 81
Good Roads magazine, 37
Good Road(s) Movement, 14, 28
Goodrich Touring Bureau, 28–29, 92
Grady, Henry W., 41
Granville, Ohio, 8
Greene, Albert, 65
Guernsey County, 38, 45, 56, 62–63, 65, 73, 79–80, 82, 87, 90; convict labor in, 37, 44, 47, 50–51, 54, 62, 66–67, 80–81; welcomes governor, 36

Haeckel, Ernst, 40, 41
Hanley, Edward W., 20
Harding, Warren G., 26, 94, 95
Harmon, Judson, 21
Hays, Will, 94
Henderson, Frank, 81
Hite Law, 25
Hogan, Timothy, 26
Hulbert, A. B., 7
Humphrey, Dudley S., 68–69
Huxley, Thomas, 40

I-70, 97
International Workers of the World (Wobblies), 94
interurbans, 8, 28, 30
Irving, Charles, 81

Jacksonburg, Ohio, 16
Jefferson, Thomas, 5, 6
Jenkins, Thomas C., 37, 47, 52, 81
Johnson, John (Cuyahoga County), 81
Johnson, John (Jefferson County), 81
Jones, William, 81
Jordan, Philip, 85
Justice, J. P., 65, 67

Kellogg, H. W., 57
Kerwick, Morgan, 81

Koko, Matt, 65
Kramer, John, 52

Lattimer, George, 28
light rail. *See* interurban
Lincoln Highway, 32–33, 50
Lore City, 50
Lowes, Dr. Joseph E., 19
Lucas, Leroy, 81

MacIntyre, John, 5
Madison, James, 5, 7
Madison, Ohio, 17
Madonna of the Trail, 98
Malthus, Thomas, 40
Marker, James R., 23, 82
Mason, Curtis, 81
Mazzola, Cassadia, 66
McAdoo, William G., 94
McCarty, Mary, 96, 101
McCarty, Vera Seiler, 96
McColloch, Elizabeth, 4
McCulloch, Allen R., 34, 52, 54, 72–73, 77, 80
McGhee, Joseph, 1, 34–36, 52
McGraw, Ed, 81
Mellet, Don, 95
Middletown, Ohio, 17
Middletown *Weekly Signal* newspaper, 17
Miller, George, 65
monogenist theory, 41
Monroe, James, 9
Montgomery, Knox, 75, 77, 78
Moore, B. V., 62
Moore, L. P., 67, 90
Moorehead, Dwight L., 66
Muskingum County, 3, 6, 25, 44, 53, 56, 63, 65, 68, 81, 89, 90; B&O railroad spur, 60; construction project in, 46–48, 52, 71, 73, 77, 82, 88; on convict labor, 51, 54, 56, 78; road project introduced in, 34–36

National Cash Register Company, 19
National Old Trails Road Association, 82, 84, 97–98
National Old Trails Road, 84, 97
National Road, 13–14, 24–26, 44, 46, 49, 52–53, 59, 61, 65, 68, 70–71, 81, 83, 87, 89–90, 98–99; as Cumberland Pike, 7, 10, 77; as Cumberland Road, 7, 84; decline, 9; "Golden Era," 7–9; modern decline, 97; as Pike, the, 2, 3, 23, 33–35, 48, 50, 54, 56, 58, 60, 62, 69, 72–73, 75, 78–80, 85, 97; post-WWII success, 86; restoration proposed, 33–38; Road founded, 7-8
National Road/Zane Grey Museum, 101
National Society of the Daughters of the American Revolution, 97–98
Neil House, 85
Neilan, John F., 18
New Concord, Ohio, 52, 60, 62, 71–72, 78, 98; final ceremonies, 75–77, 80
Newark, Ohio, 8, 23–26
Newman, Warren, 81
Niagara Falls, 83

Office of Road Inquiry, 14, 23
Ohio, 1, 85
Ohio and Erie Canal, 8
Ohio Brick Manufacturers' Association, 82
Ohio Good Roads Federation, 28, 30, 32
Ohio Highway Advisory Board, 35, 46, 48, 50–52, 54, 62, 66, 68, 71–72, 74, 75, 77–78, 80, 82, 89, 90
Ohio Highways Commission, 1
Ohio Paving Block Manufacturers Association, 75
Ohio State Penitentiary, 2, 22, 35, 45, 55, 81, 90
Ohio State Reformatory at Mansfield, 46–47, 54, 66, 78, 80; accommodations for prisoner laborers, 56–57; affected by Spanish flu, 81; agrees to send laborers to Muskingum County, 52; escapees, 65; grants paroles or releases, 71, 81; reforms, 37
Old Washington, Ohio, 33–34, 50, 73, 77, 79–80, 87
Osborne, Thomas Mott, 37

Page, Logan W., 28, 32, 84, 98
Palmer, A. Mitchell, 94
Patterson, John H., 19

Index   123

Pennsylvania House, 85
Pleasant, James, 81
polygenist theory, 40
Progressives, 14, 16, 39

Rambo, Harry M., 59
Renick, Harness, 67, 74, 79; accused of
    slow progress, 54, 69, 73; builds
    prisoner housing, 44, 50; called before
    advisory board, 74; investigated by
    state legislature, 87–90; needs more
    prison labor, 45
Reynolds, Harold, 65
Rice, Charles, 81
Roosevelt, Franklin Delano, 94
Roosevelt, Theodore, 14, 16, 20, 23

Sanders, Arthur, 81
Scales, John, 65
Sing Sing Correctional Facility, New York,
    37
Smith, Doug, 7
Smith, S. M., 90
Snouffer Brothers Construction Co., 58
Sorg, Paul J., 18, 19
Springfield, Ohio, 7, 79, 85, 98
Springfield Daily News, 19
St. Clairsville, Ohio, 8
Stewart, Luke, 81
Stout, E. E., 50
Strait, Ralph, 44, 68
Style, Richard, 65
Swords, Clinton, 65

Taft, William Howard, 16, 23
Taylor, Ed, 81
Tell, William, 65
Terman, Lewis, 41
Thomas, Preston Elmer, Ohio Peniten-
    tiary superintendent, 2, 35, 45, 50, 52,
    54; death of, 92; during Penitentiary
    fire, 90–91; hired by Cox, 22; methods
    criticized, 46; offers to build all Ohio
    roads, 70
Tibbetts, E. C., 29
tolls and toll gates, 9
Townsend, O. N., 82
Trailsend, 93
Truman, Harry, 97–98

US Council of National Defense, 1, 32, 35,
    42, 92
US Department of Agriculture, 14
US Route 40, 84–86, 97–98
Uhler, H. D., 33

Virchow, Rudolph, 40
Virginia, 39, 41, 83
Vuksic, Joe, 58, 66

Walker, Francis Amasa, 40
Walker, W. F., 49
Walton, William, 81
Wapakoneta, Ohio, 22
Washington, DC, 6, 12–13, 18, 21, 25, 28, 48,
    83, 89
Washington, John, 81
Watkins, William, 81
Wertz Law (Ohio House Bill 77), 38, 70
Wheeler, Jacob, 81
Wheeling, West Virginia, 4, 6, 7, 13, 79
White, George, 75
Williams, S. M., 28, 37
Willis, Frank B., 26–27, 35, 42, 46
Wilson, Woodrow, 23, 27, 32, 41–42, 48,
    93–94
Wiseman, Mrs. Henry, 83–84
World War I, 1, 3, 28, 87
World War II, 85, 97
WSB radio station, 95
Wyatt, Clyde, 81

Yakovich, Mike, 66
Yerkes, Robert, 41

Zane, Betty, 5
Zane, Ebenezer, 3–5, 13, 77, 98
Zane's Trace, 6–7, 98
Zanesville, Ohio, 2, 3, 4, 25, 46, 48, 49, 50,
    51, 52, 58, 59, 60, 61, 79, 84, 88, 90; cited
    for road renewal, 33; clergy visits
    camp, 56, 57; final ceremonies, 71–72,
    75–76; named, 6; National Road
    pavement, 6–7, 23–24, 26, 86
Zanesville *Times Recorder*, 59, 88, 90

Jeffrey Alan John, PhD, experienced journalism as a daily newspaper reporter, motorcycle magazine editor, and historical society public relations writer. He then taught journalism for thirty years, and he continues as a Professor Emeritus in Wright State University's Department of Communication. He is co-author with the late Frank L. Johnson of the true-crime tale *A Bird in Your Hand: A Story of Ambiguous Justice*, and author of the science fiction *Lab Rats Can't Say No: A Story in the Future*; his scholarly works include a study of the Wright Brothers' photography, and a longitudinal examination of news content in a Midwest city. He and his wife Karin Avila-John live in Dayton, Ohio's Oregon Historic District.